Pictures Tell

A Passover Haggadah

W0007467

ZION OZERI

EDITED BY
JOSHUA A. FEINBERG AND SARA WOLKENFELD
AND KEZIA RAFFEL PRIDE

With contributions by
Rabbi Dr. Joshua Berman; Dr. Mijal Bitton; Rabbi Daniel Bouskila;
Rabbi Elliot J. Cosgrove, PhD; Dr. Daniel Gordis; Yossi Klein Halevi;
Rabbi Ammiel Hirsch; Rabba Sara Hurwitz; Prof. Deborah E. Lipstadt, PhD;
Karma Lowe; Prof. Jonathan D. Sarna; David Suissa; Rachel Wahba;
and Rabbi David Wolpe

The Covenant Foundation

ANU MUSEUM OF THE JEWISH PEOPLE

gefen publishing house
JERUSALEM ◆ NEW YORK Est. 1981

WITHIN THE IMAGE

העדשה היהודית
THE JEWISH LENS

Copyright © Zion Ozeri
Jerusalem 2022/5782

All rights reserved. No part of this publication may be translated, reproduced, stored in a retrieval system or transmitted, in any form or by any means, electronic, mechanical, photocopying, recording or otherwise, without express written permission from the publishers.

Permission by the Office of Lord Sacks to quote from Rabbi Lord Jonathan Sacks, *The Chief Rabbi's Haggadah* (New York: Harper Collins, 2003), is gratefully acknowledged.

Permission to use the Sefaria Edition translation of the Haggadah text is gratefully acknowledged.

An extended version of Rabbi Daniel Bouskila, "My Judeo-Arabic Seder," was previously published in the *Jewish Journal*. It is used here with permission.

COVER DESIGN: Benjie Herskowitz/www.benherskowitz.com
COVER ILLUSTRATION: Zion Ozeri
TYPESETTING: Benjie Herskowitz
All Photographs © by Zion Ozeri

ISBN: 978-965-7801-04-8

1 3 5 7 9 8 6 4 2

Gefen Publishing House Ltd.
6 Hatzvi Street
Jerusalem 94386
Israel
972-2-538-0247
orders@gefenpublishing.com

Gefen Books
c/o Baker & Taylor Publisher Services
30 Amberwood Parkway
Ashland, Ohio 44805
516-593-1234
orders@gefenpublishing.com

www.gefenpublishing.com

Printed in Israel
Library of Congress Control Number: 2022900655

"The Exodus is the inexhaustible source of inspiration to all those who long for freedom. It taught that right was sovereign over might; that freedom and justice must belong to all, not some; that, under God, all human beings are equal; and that over all earthly powers is the supreme power, the King of Kings, who hears the cry of the oppressed and who intervenes in history to liberate slaves."

– Rabbi Lord Jonathan Sacks, *z"l, The Chief Rabbi's Haggadah*

Four Mothers, Mevaseret Zion Absorption Center, Israel, 2000

I dedicate this Haggadah to my late wife,

Ellen de Jonge-Ozeri, z"l,

whose decades-long support, advice, and love for the Jewish people

guided and inspired me.

With gratitude to my friends who stood by me over the years and supported our

mutual educational endeavors:

Alisa Doctoroff, Linda Mirels, Sandy Antignas, Ellen de Jonge-Ozeri, z"l, Shulamit

Bahat, Harlene Winnick Appleman, Joni Blinderman, and Randie Malinsky, z"l

– ZION OZERI

Preface

About This Haggadah

The Passover Seder is many things: a festive meal, a celebration of springtime, a retelling and reliving of monumental historical events, and a chance to offer praise for God's great miracles past. But beneath it all, the Seder is a symbol – a symbol of Jewish peoplehood, Jewish continuity, and Jewish unity. It is a reflection of Jewish connection across both time and space.

As we progress through the Seder ritual, we relive the moment(s) when we first became a nation – burnished in the crucibles of slavery and idolatry and strengthened by the hope and promise of redemption. We hear the voices of ancient sages and learned rabbis mingling with the stories, lessons, and recollections of our more recent ancestors – our grandparents, parents, aunts, and uncles who have joined us at the table. We taste the bitter maror and sweet charoset our forebears tasted, alongside the familiar flavors of our favorite childhood recipes.

And as we sit down to this multisensory mélange of past and present, our Jewish cousins around the world begin their own versions of this extraordinary experience. The flavors are different, the tunes unfamiliar, the decor drawn from distinct local traditions, but the experience is the same. Despite our differences, Jews the world over are connected by this annual rebirth, this realization that we are one.

This theme of Jewish peoplehood across time and space is not unique to the Seder. It also happens to be a central theme of the work of renowned photographer Zion Ozeri. Over the course of decades – and many hundreds of thousands of miles – Ozeri has sought out far-flung Jewish communities, often separated by vast ethnic, cultural, and linguistic gulfs. And yet, through his photographs, he has managed to capture what connects us all: an unbreakable bond with the past; with the customs, beliefs, and traditions that have sustained us; and with an almost tangible sense of Jewish peoplehood. A connection across time and space.

It is therefore not surprising that Ozeri's photographs blend so well with the text of the Haggadah. These texts and images speak the same language. They talk to each other.

In fact, this Haggadah is part of a long and rich tradition of illustrated and illuminated Haggadot. From the illuminated manuscripts of medieval France and Germany to the first printed Haggadot of Renaissance Italy and modern-art versions illustrated by Chagall and Shahn, the Haggadah is perhaps the most illustrated of all Jewish books. And in the most successful examples, the pictures are not mere illustrations. They are commentaries, interpretations, and explanations that give added meaning to the text. The artist's unique understanding and perspective creates a visual commentary or "midrash" – offering new insights and new opportunities for discovery.

So, too, here. The photographs contained in these pages are not mere illustrations. They are visual commentaries – "texts" in their own right – that speak to, expand on, challenge, and recontextualize the words that have been so carefully handed down through the generations. And just as each generation must see itself as having personally come out of Egypt, so too must each generation make the experience personally relevant by viewing it through a unique and uniquely relevant medium.

Reading a Photograph

While accounting for the distinct and distinctive attributes of the medium itself, a photographic "text" can, in many ways, be read like a traditional text. When we approach a Jewish text, it is common to look first for the *pshat* – literally the "simple meaning" of the words. Once we have examined the *pshat*, we move on to the *drash* – the explanation or interpretation. Finally, we take these understandings and use them to make connections – with other texts, with aspects of Jewish practice, and with broader themes of our tradition.

One can approach a visual text in much the same way. The first question we might ask is, "What do I see? What is the *pshat*, or simple reading?" Or, put another way, "What is happening here?" Once we've established the *pshat*, we can move on to the *drash*. "How do I explain or interpret what I see? What's the deeper meaning?" Finally, it's time to make connections: "How does this image connect to a particular text in the Haggadah? How does it exemplify or amplify an aspect of our Passover observance? How does it reveal, clarify, or challenge a deeper theme of our faith?"

Brief descriptions for all of the photographs in this Haggadah are provided at the end of the book, but we encourage you to explore each photograph "as is" before reading the description, so that you can approach it with fresh eyes and few preconceptions.

A Conversation

Ultimately, we hope you will explore all these texts – the written and the visual – in conversation with each other. As you make your way through the Seder service, take the time to "read" the photographs along with the Haggadah text, either to yourself or as a group. Consider what you see, what you think (or feel or understand) about what you see, and how it connects more broadly. What do the photographs have to teach the words? How do the words respond? What questions are raised by this cross-media conversation?

For some of the photographs, we have included questions that may help you get started – questions that foster closer looking, encourage reflection, or call out connections with specific texts. You'll also find QR codes linked to study sheets on the Sefaria website that offer directions for deeper exploration if you're so inclined. But don't limit yourself to the questions provided. All of the photographs have something to add to the discussion, so let them speak. Follow their lead. Let them drive the conversation.

And because every conversation becomes richer with more participants, we have included a third set of voices, in addition to the photographs and the traditional Haggadah text. Throughout the Haggadah, you'll find short entries by a variety of contemporary Jewish thinkers – personal reflections, textual clarifications, historical provocations. These bite-sized supplements, it is hoped, will add another, personal perspective to your already rich conversation. Give them the space to join in the discussion.

And now, to paraphrase the Haggadah itself, "Go forth and explore." Read the text, examine the photographs, discuss the ideas – and discover for yourself the threads that link us all together inexorably across time and space.

A Note about the Translation

The English translation in this Haggadah has been adapted with permission from the Sefaria Edition, but has been further edited for style and readability.

In an attempt to remain as true as possible to the original text of the Haggadah, the English translation retains some of the gendered forms and pronouns of the traditional Hebrew text. These formulations reflect, to a large degree, the cultures and norms of the periods in which the texts were written. You may adjust the English usage at your own Seder as you see fit to best suit your own needs and sensibilities.

הדלקת נרות
Hadlakat Nerot: Lighting Candles

בָּרוּךְ אַתָּה ה׳ אֱלֹהֵינוּ מֶלֶךְ הָעוֹלָם אֲשֶׁר קִדְּשָׁנוּ בְּמִצְוֹתָיו וְצִוָּנוּ לְהַדְלִיק נֵר שֶׁל יוֹם טוֹב.

בָּרוּךְ אַתָּה ה׳ אֱלֹהֵינוּ מֶלֶךְ הָעוֹלָם שֶׁהֶחֱיָנוּ וְקִיְּמָנוּ וְהִגִּיעָנוּ לַזְּמַן הַזֶּה.

BLESSED *are You, Lord our God, Sovereign of the universe, who has sanctified us with Your commandments and commanded us to light the holiday lights.*

BLESSED *are You, Lord our God, Sovereign of the universe, who has kept us alive, sustained us, and brought us to this season.*

The Arlene Fern School, Buenos Aires, Argentina, 2002

1

סימני הסדר
SIMANEI HASEDER: THE SEDER SEQUENCE

KADDESH: Make Kiddush   קַדֵּשׁ

URCHATZ: Wash Hands   וּרְחַץ

KARPAS: Eat the Greens   כַּרְפַּס

YACHATZ: Break the Matzah   יַחַץ

MAGGID: Tell the Story   מַגִּיד

RACHATZAH: Wash Hands   רַחְצָה

MOTZI MATZAH: Eat the Matzah   מוֹצִיא מַצָּה

MAROR: Eat the Maror   מָרוֹר

KORECH: Make a Sandwich   כּוֹרֵךְ

SHULCHAN ORECH: Enjoy the Meal   שֻׁלְחָן עוֹרֵךְ

TZAFUN: Reveal the Hidden Matzah   צָפוּן

BARECH: Bless after the Meal   בָּרֵךְ

HALLEL: Say Hallel   הַלֵּל

NIRTZAH: Conclude   נִרְצָה

לְהַדְלִיק נֵר שֶׁל יוֹם טוֹב

"To light the holiday lights…"

Holiday Lights, Mumbai, India, 2001

What idea or ideal do the holiday lights evoke in this photograph?
How does candle-lighting elevate our festival experience?
How can we bring more light into our lives and our celebrations?

Scan here for further questions and texts relating to this photograph.

קַדֵּשׁ
KADDESH: MAKE KIDDUSH

מוזגים כוס ראשונה. המצות מכוסות.

Pour the first cup. The matzot are covered.

בשבת מתחילים:

On Shabbat, begin here:

וַיְהִי עֶרֶב וַיְהִי בֹקֶר יוֹם הַשִּׁשִּׁי. וַיְכֻלּוּ הַשָּׁמַיִם וְהָאָרֶץ וְכָל־צְבָאָם. וַיְכַל אֱלֹהִים בַּיּוֹם הַשְּׁבִיעִי מְלַאכְתּוֹ אֲשֶׁר עָשָׂה וַיִּשְׁבֹּת בַּיּוֹם הַשְּׁבִיעִי מִכָּל מְלַאכְתּוֹ אֲשֶׁר עָשָׂה. וַיְבָרֶךְ אֱלֹהִים אֶת יוֹם הַשְּׁבִיעִי וַיְקַדֵּשׁ אוֹתוֹ כִּי בוֹ שָׁבַת מִכָּל־מְלַאכְתּוֹ אֲשֶׁר בָּרָא אֱלֹהִים לַעֲשׂוֹת.

THERE was evening and there was morning, the sixth day. The heaven and the earth were finished, and all their host. On the seventh day, God finished His work that He had done; and He rested on the seventh day from all His work that He had done. And God blessed the seventh day, and sanctified it, because He rested on it from all His work that He had created. (Genesis 1:31–2:3)

בחול מתחילים:

On weekdays, begin here:

בָּרוּךְ אַתָּה ה׳, אֱלֹהֵינוּ מֶלֶךְ הָעוֹלָם בּוֹרֵא פְּרִי הַגָּפֶן.

בָּרוּךְ אַתָּה ה׳, אֱלֹהֵינוּ מֶלֶךְ הָעוֹלָם אֲשֶׁר בָּחַר בָּנוּ מִכָּל־עָם וְרוֹמְמָנוּ מִכָּל־לָשׁוֹן וְקִדְּשָׁנוּ בְּמִצְוֹתָיו. וַתִּתֶּן לָנוּ ה׳ אֱלֹהֵינוּ בְּאַהֲבָה (בשבת: שַׁבָּתוֹת לִמְנוּחָה וּ) מוֹעֲדִים לְשִׂמְחָה, חַגִּים וּזְמַנִּים לְשָׂשׂוֹן, (בשבת: אֶת יוֹם הַשַּׁבָּת הַזֶּה וְ) אֶת יוֹם חַג הַמַּצוֹת הַזֶּה זְמַן חֵרוּתֵנוּ, (בשבת: בְּאַהֲבָה) מִקְרָא קֹדֶשׁ זֵכֶר לִיצִיאַת מִצְרָיִם. כִּי בָנוּ בָחַרְתָּ וְאוֹתָנוּ קִדַּשְׁתָּ מִכָּל הָעַמִּים, (בשבת: וְשַׁבָּת) וּמוֹעֲדֵי קָדְשֶׁךָ (בשבת: בְּאַהֲבָה וּבְרָצוֹן) בְּשִׂמְחָה וּבְשָׂשׂוֹן הִנְחַלְתָּנוּ.

בָּרוּךְ אַתָּה ה׳, מְקַדֵּשׁ (בשבת: הַשַּׁבָּת וְ) יִשְׂרָאֵל וְהַזְּמַנִּים.

BLESSED are You, Lord our God, Sovereign of the universe, who creates the fruit of the vine.

4

BLESSED are You, Lord our God, Sovereign of the universe, who chose us from all nations and raised us above all tongues and sanctified us with His commandments. You have given us, Lord our God, [Sabbaths for rest,] appointed times for happiness, holidays and special times for joy, [this Sabbath day, and] this Festival of Matzot, our season of freedom, [in love,] a holy assembly in memory of the exodus from Egypt. For You have chosen us and sanctified us above all nations. In Your gracious love, You granted us Your [holy Sabbath and] special times for happiness and joy.

Blessed are You, O Lord, who sanctifies [the Sabbath,] Israel, and the appointed times.

Wine Making, Tashkent, Uzbekistan, 1998

5

בָּרוּךְ אַתָּה ה׳, אֱלֹהֵינוּ מֶלֶךְ הָעוֹלָם, בּוֹרֵא מְאוֹרֵי הָאֵשׁ.

בָּרוּךְ אַתָּה ה׳, אֱלֹהֵינוּ מֶלֶךְ הָעוֹלָם הַמַּבְדִּיל בֵּין קֹדֶשׁ לְחֹל, בֵּין אוֹר לְחֹשֶׁךְ, בֵּין יִשְׂרָאֵל לָעַמִּים,
בֵּין יוֹם הַשְּׁבִיעִי לְשֵׁשֶׁת יְמֵי הַמַּעֲשֶׂה. בֵּין קְדֻשַּׁת שַׁבָּת לִקְדֻשַּׁת יוֹם טוֹב הִבְדַּלְתָּ, וְאֶת־יוֹם הַשְּׁבִיעִי
מִשֵּׁשֶׁת יְמֵי הַמַּעֲשֶׂה קִדַּשְׁתָּ. הִבְדַּלְתָּ וְקִדַּשְׁתָּ אֶת־עַמְּךָ יִשְׂרָאֵל בִּקְדֻשָּׁתֶךָ.

בָּרוּךְ אַתָּה ה׳, הַמַּבְדִּיל בֵּין קֹדֶשׁ לְקֹדֶשׁ.

BLESSED *are You, Lord our God, Sovereign of the universe, who creates the light of the fire.*

BLESSED *are You, Lord our God, Sovereign of the universe, who distinguishes between the holy and the profane, between light and darkness, between Israel and the nations, between the seventh day and the six working days. You have distinguished between the holiness of the Sabbath and the holiness of the festival day, and You have sanctified the seventh day above the six working days. You have distinguished and sanctified Your people Israel with Your holiness.*

BLESSED *are You, O Lord, who distinguishes between holy and holy.*

בָּרוּךְ אַתָּה ה׳, אֱלֹהֵינוּ מֶלֶךְ הָעוֹלָם, שֶׁהֶחֱיָנוּ וְקִיְּמָנוּ וְהִגִּיעָנוּ לַזְּמַן הַזֶּה.

BLESSED *are You, Lord our God, Sovereign of the universe, who has granted us life and sustenance and permitted us to reach this moment.*

שׁוֹתֶה בַהֲסִבַּת שְׂמֹאל וְאֵינוֹ מְבָרֵךְ בְּרָכָה אַחֲרוֹנָה.
Drink while reclining to the left.

מְקַדֵּשׁ יִשְׂרָאֵל וְהַזְּמַנִּים

"...who sanctifies Israel and the appointed times."

Synagogue, Alibag, India, 2001

What strikes you most about this photograph?
Where do you see sanctity or holiness in this photograph?
How do we sanctify the people, places, objects, or moments in our lives?
Scan here for further questions and texts relating to this photograph.

וּרְחַץ
URCHATZ: WASH HANDS

נוטלים את הידיים ואין מברכים "על נטילת ידיים".

Wash your hands but do not say the blessing on the washing of the hands.

Soup Kitchen, Buenos Aires, Argentina, 2002

כַּרְפַּס
KARPAS: EAT THE GREENS

לוקח מן הכרפס פחות מכזית – כדי שלא יתחייב בברכה אחרונה – טובל במי מלח, מברך "בורא פרי האדמה",
ומכוון לפטור בברכה גם את המרור. אוכל בלא הסבה.

Take a small piece of the greens (so that you will not need to say the blessing after eating it), dip it into the salt water,
and recite the blessing below. This blessing will also be for the bitter herbs later on. Eat without reclining.

בָּרוּךְ אַתָּה ה', אֱלֹהֵינוּ מֶלֶךְ הָעוֹלָם, בּוֹרֵא פְּרִי הָאֲדָמָה.

BLESSED are You, Lord our God, Sovereign of the universe, who creates the fruit of the earth.

Farmer, Eastern Galilee, Israel, 1987

9

My Judeo-Arabic Seder

"Our entire Passover Seder is translated into Arabic," I used to tell my Ashkenazi friends in school. "Arabic?" they responded in bewilderment. "That's so weird! How could you translate a Seder into Arabic?" While Ashkenazi Jews might find Arabic an unwelcome guest at their Seder, for my family, Arabic was a central part of our French- and Arabic-speaking Sephardic-Moroccan home in Los Angeles every day, and certainly on Passover. Ashkenazim hear the tune of "Mah Nishtanah" and say, "Now we feel like it's Passover." For my family, our Judeo-Moroccan equivalent of that sounded like this:

Haq'da qssam l'lah lb'har âla tnass l'treq 'hin khrzeu
zdoud'na min massar, âla yed sid'na oun'bina moussa ben amram
haq'da n'khrzeu min had l'galouth amen ken yehi ratson.

My father chanted this beautiful text during Yachatz, as he split the middle matzah. It's not a formal part of the Haggadah's text (hence you won't find it in your Haggadah); rather, it's one of the beautiful oral traditions of Moroccan Jews, passed down – in the spirit of Passover – from generation to generation (my kids do it to this day).

For me, this Judeo-Arabic chant evoked images of my great-grandfather Rabbi Yosef Pinto sitting at his Seder in Marrakech, dressed in a *jalabiya* with a scarf on his head, breaking the middle matzah and recounting the exodus to my father and the other children at the table. Because it's in Arabic, *Haq'da Qssam L'lah* reminded me what my father always told me – that Moroccan Jewry had cordial relations with their Muslim neighbors. Thank God, we are seeing that return today.

Throughout my childhood, we never asked what this chant meant. The language and rhythm were so rich that the emotional meaning far exceeded a literal translation. When my father passed away, I searched for the translation of *Haq'da Qssam L'lah*, and here is what I found:

"This is how the Holy One, blessed be He, split the sea into twelve separate paths, when our ancestors left Egypt, through the leadership of our master and prophet, Moses son of Amram, of blessed memory. Just as God redeemed them and saved them from harsh labors and brought them to freedom, so too may the Holy One, blessed be He, redeem us for the sake of His great name, and let us say Amen."

As nice as it is to have the translation, it sounds – and feels – so much better in the original.

– Rabbi Daniel Bouskila

יַחַץ
YACHATZ: BREAK THE MATZAH

חותך את המצה האמצעית לשניים, ומצפין את הנתח הגדול לאפיקומן.
מגלה את המצות, מגביה את הקערה ואומר בקול רם:

Split the middle matzah in two and hide the larger piece to use for the afikomen.
Uncover the matzot, raise the Seder plate, and say out loud:

הָא לַחְמָא עַנְיָא דִּי אֲכָלוּ אַבְהָתָנָא בְּאַרְעָא דְמִצְרָיִם. כָּל דִּכְפִין יֵיתֵי וְיֵיכֹל, כָּל דִּצְרִיךְ יֵיתֵי וְיִפְסַח. הָשַׁתָּא הָכָא, לְשָׁנָה הַבָּאָה בְּאַרְעָא דְיִשְׂרָאֵל. הָשַׁתָּא עַבְדֵי, לְשָׁנָה הַבָּאָה בְּנֵי חוֹרִין.

THIS is the bread of poverty that our ancestors ate in the land of Egypt. All who are hungry, come and eat; all who are in need, come and partake of the Pesach sacrifice. Now we are here – next year we will be in the land of Israel; this year we are enslaved – next year we will be free people.

Soup Kitchen, New York City, New York, 1992

Ha Lachma Anya

"This is the bread of affliction that our ancestors ate in the land of Egypt." Baked into the most famous item on the Seder table – matzah – is an age-old question. Does the matzah remind us of the Israelites' impoverished condition or of their hurried departure from Egypt and the dough that did not have a chance to rise? Is the matzah a symbol of our servitude or our liberation?

Not only matzah, but several items on the Seder plate carry a double meaning. The salt water reminds us on the one hand of the tears shed by the slaves. On the other hand, only free people can dip their food with leisure. At one and the same time, the charoset is a reminder of the mortar used to build the pyramids and also sweetens the bitterness of the maror.

The double meaning of the Passover symbols teaches us a lesson. We are called on to be transformed by the Seder while at the same time remaining ourselves. The difference between slavery and freedom is not so much a change of substance as of attitude. If nothing else, the Seder demands that we see ourselves and others from a different point of view.

Above all, *ha lachma anya* invites all who are hungry, physically and spiritually, to the possibilities of the Seder. This year we may be slaves; next year each one of us can be free.

– Rabbi Elliot J. Cosgrove, PhD

כָּל דִּכְפִין יֵיתֵי וְיֵיכֹל

"All who are hungry, come and eat..."

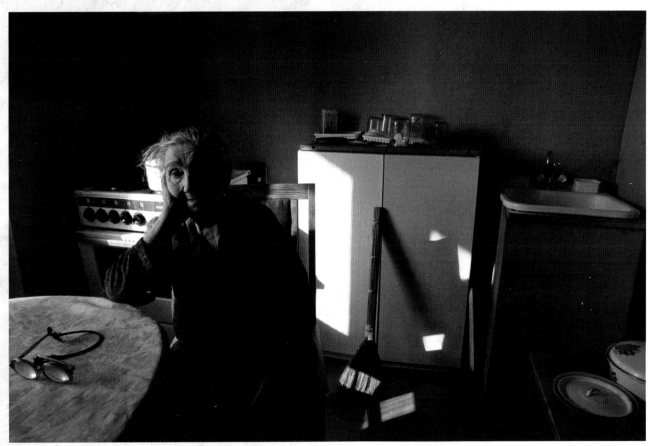

Kitchen, Kiev, Ukraine, 1991

What do you notice about this woman and her setting?

What do you imagine she might be thinking or feeling?

How do you connect this photograph with the themes of the *ha lachma* prayer?

Scan here for further questions and texts relating to this photograph.

15

מַגִּיד
MAGGID: TELL THE STORY

מה נשתנה
Mah Nishtanah: Four Questions

מסיר את הקערה מעל השולחן. מוזגים כוס שנייה. ילד שואל:
Remove the Seder plate from the table and pour a second cup of wine. The youngest then asks:

מַה נִּשְׁתַּנָּה הַלַּיְלָה הַזֶּה מִכָּל הַלֵּילוֹת?

שֶׁבְּכָל הַלֵּילוֹת אָנוּ אוֹכְלִין חָמֵץ וּמַצָּה, הַלַּיְלָה הַזֶּה – כֻּלּוֹ מַצָּה.

שֶׁבְּכָל הַלֵּילוֹת אָנוּ אוֹכְלִין שְׁאָר יְרָקוֹת – הַלַּיְלָה הַזֶּה (כֻּלּוֹ) מָרוֹר.

שֶׁבְּכָל הַלֵּילוֹת אֵין אָנוּ מַטְבִּילִין אֲפִילוּ פַּעַם אֶחָת – הַלַּיְלָה הַזֶּה שְׁתֵּי פְעָמִים.

שֶׁבְּכָל הַלֵּילוֹת אָנוּ אוֹכְלִין בֵּין יוֹשְׁבִין וּבֵין מְסֻבִּין – הַלַּיְלָה הַזֶּה כֻּלָּנוּ מְסֻבִּין.

WHAT makes this night different from all other nights?

ON all other nights, we eat bread and matzah; why tonight only matzah?

ON all other nights, we eat different kinds of vegetables; why tonight only bitter herbs?

ON all other nights, we don't dip our food even once; why tonight do we do it twice?

ON all other nights, we eat either sitting or reclining; why tonight do we all recline?

While the Haggadah text remains virtually unchanged throughout the world, diverse communities bring their own customs and melodies to the Seder ritual.
Scan here to hear how different Jewish communities sing *"Mah Nishtanah."*

Scan here to hear a Yemenite version.

16

Brooklyn,
USA, 1996

Why Build a Meal around Questions?

Unlike a good answer, a good question is inexhaustible. We return to the same question year after year and discover new possibilities, avenues, explorations. Why is this night different? Not only because it is different from every other night, but because it is different from last year when we asked the same question. An answer gives the satisfaction of a resolving chord. A question gives the anticipatory excitement of an opening note.

In Deuteronomy (32:7), we are instructed to ask our elders. The questions of the Seder are put into the mouth of the youngest. But everyone comes along to answer – the Torah, the rabbis, and the Seder participants collaborate to tell the story with its terrors and miracles and liberations. A deep question requires a chorus of responses; questions open worlds.

The Talmud teaches that Elijah, when he arrives to announce the coming of the messiah, will answer all the questions the Talmudic rabbis could not definitely determine for themselves. What a tradition, that anticipates the Messianic time so that we can ask our questions! The Seder tells us to be sensitive to the changes, beauty, and anguish of the world, not because we will always understand it, but to evoke our wonder and ask why it must be so. Judaism is here to interrogate the world, to learn its secrets by the simple, powerful tool of the question. What could be more simple, or more sacred?

– Rabbi David Wolpe

מַה נִּשְׁתַּנָּה הַלַּיְלָה הַזֶּה
"What makes this night different..."

Cave, Haidan A-Sham, Yemen, 1992

What questions do you have about this photograph? What piques your curiosity?

How does this image connect with the *mah nishtanah* text?

What role do questions play in your religious or spiritual life?

Scan here for further questions and texts relating to this photograph.

19

מא כבר
Ma Chabar

Growing up in Israel with parents who were immigrants from Yemen, we children always looked forward to the holiday of Passover. It was all fun for us – since cleaning the house, changing over the dishes, and cooking were not chores we, the young ones, much participated in. It was a time when my parents, with their meager means, bought each one of us new clothes and shoes – something that rarely happened in a family of twelve.

At the Seder, one of the youngest of us was given a special task (every year or two it was assigned to the next child down the line who had learned to read): to read in Judeo-Arabic an abbreviated version of the Haggadah's exodus story, known as "Ma Chabar." This custom was enacted so that Seder participants who were not well versed in Hebrew would be able to understand and perform the mitzvah of the Haggadah – the telling of the exodus story.

– Zion Ozeri

Here's a link to Ma Chabar in Arabic.

The text of Ma Chabar is translated into Hebrew and English below:

מה עניין הלילה הזה מכל הלילות? יצאו סבינו ואבותינו ממצרים, בית העבדים.

מה היו עושים [שם]? היו מערבבים תבן בלבנים ולבנים בתבן, עבור מי?

עבור פרעה הרשע הגמור, אשר ראשו דומה למפלצת ופיו [גדול] כפי התנור, והוריד ה' על המצרים

הדם והצפרדעים והכינים והפרעושים והערוב והדבר והשחין והברד והארבה והחושך ומות הבכורות

ואפילו זקנה אחת, עליה יחולו אלף קללות, היה לה אליל מבצק – נכנס הכלב ואכלו וצעקה כל הלילה.

והייתה צעקה גדולה בכל ארץ מצרים מה שנאמר "כי אין בית אשר אין שם מת". הוציאם ה' ביד חזקה ובזרוע נטויה ובשפטים גדולים ובאותות ובמופתים.

WHAT *is the meaning of this night apart from all nights? Our elders and ancestors left Egypt, the house of slavery.*

WHAT *did they do there? They were mixing mortar for bricks.*

FOR *whom? For Pharaoh, the evil, whose head looked like a monster, and whose mouth was big as an oven.*

AND *God brought upon the Egyptians the blood, frogs, lice, wild animals, pestilence, boils, hail, locusts, darkness, and the slaying of the firstborn.*

AND *even one very old woman, a thousand curses upon her, had an idol made of dough – the dog came in and ate it, and she was shouting the whole night. There was great crying all over Egypt, as the verse says, "For there was not a house without someone dead."*

THE *Lord, our God, took us out from there with a strong hand and an outstretched arm.*

עבדים היינו
Avadim Hayinu: We Were Enslaved

מחזיר את הקערה אל השולחן. המצות תהיינה מגולות בשעת אמירת ההגדה.

Return the Seder plate to the table. The matzot should be uncovered during the reading of the Haggadah.

עֲבָדִים הָיִינוּ לְפַרְעֹה בְּמִצְרַיִם, וַיּוֹצִיאֵנוּ ה' אֱלֹהֵינוּ מִשָּׁם בְּיָד חֲזָקָה וּבִזְרֹעַ נְטוּיָה. וְאִלּוּ לֹא הוֹצִיא הַקָּדוֹשׁ בָּרוּךְ הוּא אֶת אֲבוֹתֵינוּ מִמִּצְרַיִם, הֲרֵי אָנוּ וּבָנֵינוּ וּבְנֵי בָנֵינוּ מְשֻׁעְבָּדִים הָיִינוּ לְפַרְעֹה בְּמִצְרָיִם. וַאֲפִילוּ כֻּלָּנוּ חֲכָמִים כֻּלָּנוּ נְבוֹנִים כֻּלָּנוּ זְקֵנִים כֻּלָּנוּ יוֹדְעִים אֶת הַתּוֹרָה מִצְוָה עָלֵינוּ לְסַפֵּר בִּיצִיאַת מִצְרָיִם. וְכָל הַמַּרְבֶּה לְסַפֵּר בִּיצִיאַת מִצְרַיִם הֲרֵי זֶה מְשֻׁבָּח.

WE were enslaved to Pharaoh in the land of Egypt. The Lord, our God, took us out from there with a strong hand and an outstretched arm. And if the Holy One, blessed be He, had not taken our ancestors from Egypt, we and our children and our children's children would be enslaved to Pharaoh in Egypt. And even if we were all sages, all discerning, all elders, all knowledgeable about the Torah, it would be a commandment for us to tell the story of the exodus from Egypt. And anyone who expands on the telling of the story of the exodus from Egypt – he is worthy of praise.

While the Haggadah text remains virtually unchanged throughout the world, diverse communities bring their own customs and melodies to the Seder ritual.

Scan here to hear how different Jewish communities sing "Avadim Hayinu."

עֲבָדִים הָיִינוּ
"We were enslaved..."

Let My People Go, New York City, USA, 1987

How does our history as an enslaved people inform our experiences as Jews today?
What types of slavery do we encounter in today's world?
What responsibilities do we have toward the enslaved?

Freedom

Freedom is a process. Moving out of Mitzrayim (Egypt), the narrow spaces, is a journey we are mandated to take.

In my family, fleeing Mitzrayim was concretized. My father left Egypt after witnessing Hitler's *Mein Kampf* selling out in Cairo's bookstores in 1939. He had to let go of ties to his native land going back generations upon generations. My mother fled Iraq after the Farhud when mobs descended on Baghdad's Jews in 1941.

I grew up stateless in India and Japan – my parents were my country, Jews my nationality, Zionism my creed, Israel my homeland. Resilience our dance.

So why worry about the narrow spaces? We are out of Mitzrayim, our homeland has been restored, we have passports.

Freedom involves our personal journey through narrow spaces – our fears that keep us stuck and limit us from expanding. On Pesach, we embrace freedom as individuals and as a people. Together, we remember.

– Rachel Wahba

Honorable Discharge,
Ben Gurion Airport,
Israel, 1992

מעשה שהיה בבני ברק
Ma'aseh she'Hayah b'Bnei Brak:
It Happened in Bnei Brak

Study Group, Seattle, Washington, USA, 2009

מַעֲשֶׂה בְּרַבִּי אֱלִיעֶזֶר וְרַבִּי יְהוֹשֻׁעַ וְרַבִּי אֶלְעָזָר בֶּן־עֲזַרְיָה וְרַבִּי עֲקִיבָא וְרַבִּי טַרְפוֹן שֶׁהָיוּ מְסֻבִּין בִּבְנֵי־בְרַק וְהָיוּ מְסַפְּרִים בִּיצִיאַת מִצְרַיִם כָּל־אוֹתוֹ הַלַּיְלָה, עַד שֶׁבָּאוּ תַלְמִידֵיהֶם וְאָמְרוּ לָהֶם רַבּוֹתֵינוּ הִגִּיעַ זְמַן קְרִיאַת שְׁמַע שֶׁל שַׁחֲרִית.

אָמַר רַבִּי אֶלְעָזָר בֶּן־עֲזַרְיָה הֲרֵי אֲנִי כְּבֶן שִׁבְעִים שָׁנָה וְלֹא זָכִיתִי שֶׁתֵּאָמֵר יְצִיאַת מִצְרַיִם בַּלֵּילוֹת עַד שֶׁדְּרָשָׁהּ בֶּן זוֹמָא, שֶׁנֶּאֱמַר, לְמַעַן תִּזְכֹּר אֶת יוֹם צֵאתְךָ מֵאֶרֶץ מִצְרַיִם כֹּל יְמֵי חַיֶּיךָ. יְמֵי חַיֶּיךָ הַיָּמִים. כֹּל יְמֵי חַיֶּיךָ הַלֵּילוֹת. וַחֲכָמִים אוֹמְרִים יְמֵי חַיֶּיךָ הָעוֹלָם הַזֶּה. כֹּל יְמֵי חַיֶּיךָ לְהָבִיא לִימוֹת הַמָּשִׁיחַ.

IT happened that Rabbi Eliezer, Rabbi Yehoshua, Rabbi Elazar ben Azariah, Rabbi Akiva, and Rabbi Tarfon were reclining in Bnei Brak and telling the story of the exodus from Egypt that whole night – until their students came and said to them, "Our teachers, the time has come to recite the morning Shema."

RABBI Elazar ben Azariah said, "Behold I am like a man of seventy years, and I have not merited to understand why the exodus from Egypt should be said at night until Ben Zoma explained it, as it is stated, 'In order that you remember the day you left the land of Egypt all the days of your life' (Deuteronomy 16:3). 'The days of your life' refers to the days; 'all the days of your life' refers to the nights as well." But the Sages say, "'the days of your life' refers to this world; 'all the days of your life' refers to the days of the messiah as well."

Sunrise Shema, Sde Boker Israel, 2003

All the Days of Your Life

Liberty dies in two ways. The first is by foreign invasion. Internal neglect is more common. A thousand cuts, small successive compromises, gradually eat away the delicate fabric of freedom. Once even one thread rips, if it remains unrepaired, the hole expands until it is too late.

For this reason, the Haggadah's central obsession is to remind us to tell the story of freedom. Tell it all the time, day and night. Personalize it. You were there. Remember the day of redemption. Remember that day the entire day. Night is part of the day. Tell the story at night as well.

Oppression is easy to forget when you are basking in the sunlight of freedom. Liberty dies in clear sight, during the day, by neglect. So you must tell the story in daytime. If you are enduring oppression, never lose hope. The dawn will rise again. So tell the story of freedom even during the long night of your oppression.

Those who take liberty for granted, when the sun is shining on them, will lose it. Those who don't tell the story of freedom, even in the darkness of their oppression, will never see the sunrise of a new day.

– Rabbi Ammiel Hirsch

כנגד ארבעה בנים
K'neged Arba'ah Banim: About Four Children

בָּרוּךְ הַמָּקוֹם, בָּרוּךְ הוּא, בָּרוּךְ שֶׁנָּתַן תּוֹרָה לְעַמּוֹ יִשְׂרָאֵל, בָּרוּךְ הוּא. כְּנֶגֶד אַרְבָּעָה בָנִים דִּבְּרָה תּוֹרָה: אֶחָד חָכָם, וְאֶחָד רָשָׁע, וְאֶחָד תָּם, וְאֶחָד שֶׁאֵינוֹ יוֹדֵעַ לִשְׁאוֹל.

חָכָם מָה הוּא אוֹמֵר? מָה הָעֵדוֹת וְהַחֻקִּים וְהַמִּשְׁפָּטִים אֲשֶׁר צִוָּה ה' אֱלֹהֵינוּ אֶתְכֶם. וְאַף אַתָּה אֱמוֹר לוֹ כְּהִלְכוֹת הַפֶּסַח: אֵין מַפְטִירִין אַחַר הַפֶּסַח אֲפִיקוֹמָן.

רָשָׁע מָה הוּא אוֹמֵר? מָה הָעֲבוֹדָה הַזֹּאת לָכֶם. לָכֶם – וְלֹא לוֹ. וּלְפִי שֶׁהוֹצִיא אֶת עַצְמוֹ מִן הַכְּלָל כָּפַר בְּעִקָּר. וְאַף אַתָּה הַקְהֵה אֶת שִׁנָּיו וֶאֱמוֹר לוֹ: "בַּעֲבוּר זֶה עָשָׂה ה' לִי בְּצֵאתִי מִמִּצְרָיִם". לִי וְלֹא לוֹ. אִלּוּ הָיָה שָׁם, לֹא הָיָה נִגְאָל.

תָּם מָה הוּא אוֹמֵר? מַה זֹּאת? וְאָמַרְתָּ אֵלָיו "בְּחוֹזֶק יָד הוֹצִיאָנוּ ה' מִמִּצְרַיִם מִבֵּית עֲבָדִים".

וְשֶׁאֵינוֹ יוֹדֵעַ לִשְׁאוֹל – אַתְּ פְּתַח לוֹ, שֶׁנֶּאֱמַר, וְהִגַּדְתָּ לְבִנְךָ בַּיּוֹם הַהוּא לֵאמֹר, בַּעֲבוּר זֶה עָשָׂה ה' לִי בְּצֵאתִי מִמִּצְרָיִם.

BLESSED is the Eternal One; blessed is He. Blessed is the One who gave the Torah to His people Israel; blessed is He. About four children the Torah spoke: a wise one, a wicked one, a simple one, and one who doesn't know how to ask a question.

THE wise one – what does he say? "What are these testimonies, statutes, and rulings that the Lord our God commanded you?" (Deuteronomy 6:20). And you will say to him, according to the laws of the Pesach sacrifice, "We may not add an afikomen after the Pesach sacrifice" (Mishnah Pesachim 10:8).

THE wicked one – what does he say? "What is this service to you?" (Exodus 12:26). "To you" and not to him. And since he excluded himself from the community, he denied an essential principle. Therefore, you will blunt his teeth and say to him, "It is on account of what the Lord did for me when I left Egypt" (Exodus 13:8). "For me" and not for him. If he had been there, he would not have been saved.

THE simple one – what does he say? "What is this?" (Exodus 13:14). And you will say to him, "With the strength of His hand the Lord took us out of Egypt, from the house of slavery" (Exodus 13:14).

AND the one who doesn't know how to ask – you will open the conversation for him, as it is stated, "You will speak to your child on that day, saying, on account of what the Lord did for me when I left Egypt" (Exodus 13:8).

The "Evil" Child

There is a paradox at the heart of the story of the child the Haggadah calls "evil." What marks this child as "evil" rather than merely rebellious is that he leaves no room for discussion. His mocking tone is rhetorical, not inquisitive: he is the only one of the four children who is not really asking a question but making a statement. And yet, he is proclaiming his exclusion while still sitting at the table. He hasn't gotten up and left. That may well happen later; for now, though, he remains among us.

Still, the Haggadah instructs us to reciprocate his contempt and treat him as an outcast: "Set his teeth on edge" – perhaps for the sake of the siblings who are eavesdropping on the exchange.

That approach seems incomplete.

In our time, we are confronting the reemergence of the "evil child," who rejects the fundamental justness and legitimacy of our story, especially of the Jewish return home. Some anti-Zionist Jews have even organized into a movement that collaborates with those seeking our destruction. In so doing, they have left the table.

And so, with a pained heart, we must rebuke them and even reciprocate their contempt. (After all, the siblings are eavesdropping...) But at the same time, we must also convey this message: You are our children. You belong among us. We miss you at the table and await your return.

– Yossi Klein Halevi

כְּנֶגֶד אַרְבָּעָה בָנִים
"About four children..."

Nursery School, Santiago, Chile, 2002

What attitudes or attributes might you ascribe to each of these four children, based on their expressions?

What can't you tell from the photograph?

Do you think children can really be as neatly categorized as the Haggadah seems to suggest?

Scan here for further questions and texts relating to this photograph.

The Secret, Mevaseret Zion
Absorption Center, Israel,
1990

יָכוֹל מֵרֹאשׁ חוֹדֶשׁ
Yachol me'Rosh Chodesh: Perhaps from Rosh Chodesh

יָכוֹל מֵרֹאשׁ חֹדֶשׁ? תַּלְמוּד לוֹמַר בַּיּוֹם הַהוּא. אִי בַּיּוֹם הַהוּא יָכוֹל מִבְּעוֹד יוֹם? תַּלְמוּד לוֹמַר בַּעֲבוּר זֶה –
בַּעֲבוּר זֶה לֹא אָמַרְתִּי, אֶלָּא בְּשָׁעָה שֶׁיֵּשׁ מַצָּה וּמָרוֹר מֻנָּחִים לְפָנֶיךָ.

ONE could assume that we must recount the exodus starting at the beginning of the month. Therefore, the Torah says "on that day" [to indicate Passover]. But "on that day" could lead one to believe that only daytime is meant. Therefore, the Torah says "on account of this." "On account of this" teaches us that you don't tell the story except at the moment when matzah and maror sit before you [on Passover eve].

מַתְּחִלָּה עוֹבְדֵי עֲבוֹדָה זָרָה הָיוּ אֲבוֹתֵינוּ
Ovdei Avodah Zarah Hayu Avoteinu:
Our Ancestors Were Idol Worshipers

מַתְּחִלָּה עוֹבְדֵי עֲבוֹדָה זָרָה הָיוּ אֲבוֹתֵינוּ, וְעַכְשָׁיו קֵרְבָנוּ הַמָּקוֹם לַעֲבוֹדָתוֹ, שֶׁנֶּאֱמַר: וַיֹּאמֶר יְהוֹשֻׁעַ
אֶל־כָּל־הָעָם, כֹּה אָמַר ה' אֱלֹהֵי יִשְׂרָאֵל: בְּעֵבֶר הַנָּהָר יָשְׁבוּ אֲבוֹתֵיכֶם מֵעוֹלָם, תֶּרַח אֲבִי אַבְרָהָם
וַאֲבִי נָחוֹר, וַיַּעַבְדוּ אֱלֹהִים אֲחֵרִים. וָאֶקַּח אֶת־אֲבִיכֶם אֶת־אַבְרָהָם מֵעֵבֶר הַנָּהָר וָאוֹלֵךְ אוֹתוֹ בְּכָל־
אֶרֶץ כְּנָעַן, וָאַרְבֶּה אֶת־זַרְעוֹ וָאֶתֶּן לוֹ אֶת־יִצְחָק, וָאֶתֵּן לְיִצְחָק אֶת־יַעֲקֹב וְאֶת־עֵשָׂו. וָאֶתֵּן לְעֵשָׂו
אֶת־הַר שֵׂעִיר לָרֶשֶׁת אֹתוֹ, וְיַעֲקֹב וּבָנָיו יָרְדוּ מִצְרָיִם.

בָּרוּךְ שׁוֹמֵר הַבְטָחָתוֹ לְיִשְׂרָאֵל, בָּרוּךְ הוּא. שֶׁהַקָּדוֹשׁ בָּרוּךְ הוּא חִשַּׁב אֶת־הַקֵּץ, לַעֲשׂוֹת כְּמוֹ שֶׁאָמַר
לְאַבְרָהָם אָבִינוּ בִּבְרִית בֵּין הַבְּתָרִים, שֶׁנֶּאֱמַר: וַיֹּאמֶר לְאַבְרָם, יָדֹעַ תֵּדַע כִּי־גֵר יִהְיֶה זַרְעֲךָ בְּאֶרֶץ לֹא לָהֶם,
וַעֲבָדוּם וְעִנּוּ אֹתָם אַרְבַּע מֵאוֹת שָׁנָה. וְגַם אֶת־הַגּוֹי אֲשֶׁר יַעֲבֹדוּ דָּן אָנֹכִי וְאַחֲרֵי־כֵן יֵצְאוּ בִּרְכֻשׁ גָּדוֹל.

IN the beginning, our ancestors were idol worshipers. And now, the Eternal One has brought us close to worship Him, as it is stated, "Yehoshua said to the people, so said the Lord, God of Israel, 'Across the river your ancestors always dwelled, Terach the father of Avraham and the father of Nachor, and they worshiped other gods. I took your father, Avraham, from across the river and I led him throughout the land of Canaan, and I increased his seed and I gave him Yitzchak. And I gave to Yitzchak Ya'akov and Esav; and I gave to Esav Mount Seir as an inheritance. And Ya'akov and his sons went down to Egypt'" (Joshua 24:2–4)

BLESSED *is the One who keeps His promise to Israel; blessed is He. The Holy One, blessed is He, calculated the end of the exile, to do as He had said to Avraham our father in the Covenant between the Pieces, as it is stated, "And He said to Avram, 'You should surely know that your descendants will be strangers in a land that is not theirs, and they will be enslaved and afflicted for four hundred years. And I will judge the nation they are to serve, and afterwards they will leave with great wealth'" (Genesis 15:13–14).*

Blessings for the Circumcised, Mexico City, Mexico, 2004

Toward Redemption

The Seder night is about teaching. "And you shall teach them to your children," the Haggadah quotes the Torah as saying (Deuteronomy 6:7). And what better way is there to teach than to begin with a question, or with four questions, for that matter? So to get the conversation going, we begin with someone, usually a child, asking "Why is this night different?"

But if that's the question, what is the answer? Why is this night different, after all? How can it be that all of us know the questions, but have a harder time saying what the Haggadah's answer is? Perhaps that is because the Haggadah gives us two very different answers.

The first answer comes immediately after the Four Questions, in the paragraph known as "*avadim hayinu*" (we were slaves to Pharaoh in Egypt). This night is different because we both celebrate and commemorate our liberation from Egyptian slavery. Once we were slaves, and now we are not. Sounds simple, no? But wait! Pages later, after the Four Children and many other passages we're familiar with, comes a second answer. Here the Haggadah says, "*ovdei avodah zarah hayu avoteinu*" (our ancestors were idol worshippers). If the first answer is about physical redemption, the second is about spiritual or intellectual redemption. So, which is officially the Haggadah's answer?

That debate goes back thousands of years. Already in the Talmud, two third-century sages, Rav and Shmuel, had the same dispute. They had a tradition that in reciting the Passover story, we should begin with shame and move toward the glory of redemption. But what's the "shame" with which we should begin?

Here's what the Talmud tells us: "It was taught in the Mishnah that the father begins his answer with disgrace and concludes with glory. The Gemara asks: What is the meaning of the term 'with disgrace'? Rav said that one should begin by saying: At first our forefathers were idol worshippers, before concluding with words of glory. And Shmuel said: The disgrace with which one should begin his answer is: We were slaves" (*Pesachim* 116a).

We might be tempted to ask which is right or which is more important, but the bewildering world in which we now live should remind us that both Rav and Shmuel were right; without both of their visions, we can't live lives that are worth living.

Though a very few people, such as Natan Sharansky (a great Jewish hero who survived years in a Soviet prison), are able to make meaning out of their imprisonment, most of us could not. We need to be free – physically free to live where and how we wish – to fashion lives that seem to us to matter, that are worth living. Were we to be faced with a choice, then, "spiritual" liberation might seem less important.

What Rav meant by his answer, of course, was that a people who were once idolators and then marched from Egypt to the revelation at Mount Sinai were liberated not only by the end of slavery but also by discovering God. Yet we can learn more from Rav, especially in these times. If we have learned anything in recent years, it is that intellectual enslavement – to falsehoods, to baseless ideologies, to demagogic figures – not only enslaves our minds and souls but could also end our physical freedom as well.

The challenge for us at the Seder is to teach our children the wondrous story of the Israelites' escape from Egypt and their transformation into the Jewish people. After the Seder, though, our ongoing challenge is to live lives worthy of both Rav and Shmuel, lives in which we celebrate and never take for granted our physical freedom, all the while keenly aware that idolatries of all sorts are no less a threat to our freedom than were the pharaohs of old.

– **Dr. Daniel Gordis**

מכסה המצה ומגביה את הכוס בידו, ואומר:

Cover the matzah, lift up the cup, and say:

וְהִיא שֶׁעָמְדָה לַאֲבוֹתֵינוּ וְלָנוּ. שֶׁלֹּא אֶחָד בִּלְבָד עָמַד עָלֵינוּ לְכַלּוֹתֵנוּ, אֶלָּא שֶׁבְּכָל דּוֹר וָדוֹר עוֹמְדִים עָלֵינוּ לְכַלּוֹתֵנוּ, וְהַקָּדוֹשׁ בָּרוּךְ הוּא מַצִּילֵנוּ מִיָּדָם.

AND *it is this [the promise] that sustained our ancestors and us. For there has not been just one who has stood against us to destroy us; rather, in each generation, many stand against us to destroy us. But the Holy One, blessed is He, rescues us from their hand.*

Bookcase, Plovdiv, Bulgaria, 2000

 While the Haggadah text remains virtually unchanged throughout the world, diverse communities bring their own customs and melodies to the Seder ritual.
Scan here to hear how different Jewish communities sing "V'hi She'amdah."

39

ארמי אובד אבי

Arami Oved Avi: An Aramean Was Destroying My Father

יניח הכוס מידו ויגלה את המצות.
Put down the cup and uncover the matzah.

צֵא וּלְמַד מַה בִּקֵּשׁ לָבָן הָאֲרַמִּי לַעֲשׂוֹת לְיַעֲקֹב אָבִינוּ: שֶׁפַּרְעֹה לֹא גָזַר אֶלָּא עַל הַזְּכָרִים, וְלָבָן בִּקֵּשׁ לַעֲקֹר אֶת־הַכֹּל. שֶׁנֶּאֱמַר: אֲרַמִּי אֹבֵד אָבִי, וַיֵּרֶד מִצְרַיְמָה וַיָּגָר שָׁם בִּמְתֵי מְעָט, וַיְהִי שָׁם לְגוֹי גָּדוֹל, עָצוּם וָרָב.

GO out and learn what Lavan the Aramean sought to do to Ya'akov, our father; for Pharaoh only pronounced a death sentence on the males, but Lavan sought to uproot all. As it is stated, "An Aramean was destroying my father, and he went down to Egypt and resided there with a small number; but he became there a nation – great, powerful, and numerous" (Deuteronomy 26:5).

"וַיֵּרֶד מִצְרַיְמָה" – אָנוּס עַל פִּי הַדִּבּוּר.

"וַיָּגָר שָׁם" – מְלַמֵּד שֶׁלֹּא יָרַד יַעֲקֹב אָבִינוּ לְהִשְׁתַּקֵּעַ בְּמִצְרַיִם אֶלָּא לָגוּר שָׁם, שֶׁנֶּאֱמַר: וַיֹּאמְרוּ אֶל־פַּרְעֹה, לָגוּר בָּאָרֶץ בָּאנוּ, כִּי אֵין מִרְעֶה לַצֹּאן אֲשֶׁר לַעֲבָדֶיךָ, כִּי כָבֵד הָרָעָב בְּאֶרֶץ כְּנָעַן. וְעַתָּה יֵשְׁבוּ־נָא עֲבָדֶיךָ בְּאֶרֶץ גֹּשֶׁן.

"AND he went down to Egypt" – helpless on account of the word [in which God told Avraham that his descendants would have to go into exile].

"AND he resided there" – this teaches that Ya'akov, our father, didn't go down to settle in Egypt, but rather to reside there, as it is stated, "And they said to Pharaoh, 'To reside in the land have we come, since there is not enough pasture for your servant's flocks, since the famine weighs heavily in the land of Canaan. And now please grant that your servants may dwell in the Land of Goshen'" (Genesis 47:4).

Tourists, Negev, Israel, 2005

"בְּמַתֵי" מְעַט" – כְּמָה שֶׁנֶּאֱמַר: בְּשִׁבְעִים נֶפֶשׁ יָרְדוּ אֲבוֹתֶיךָ מִצְרָיְמָה, וְעַתָּה שָׂמְךָ ה' אֱלֹהֶיךָ כְּכוֹכְבֵי הַשָּׁמַיִם לָרֹב.

"וַיְהִי שָׁם לְגוֹי" – מְלַמֵּד בְּהָיוּ יִשְׂרָאֵל מְצֻיָּנִים שָׁם.

"גָּדוֹל עָצוּם" – כְּמָה שֶׁנֶּאֱמַר: וּבְנֵי יִשְׂרָאֵל פָּרוּ וַיִּשְׁרְצוּ וַיִּרְבּוּ וַיַּעַצְמוּ בִּמְאֹד מְאֹד, וַתִּמָּלֵא הָאָרֶץ אֹתָם.

"וָרָב" – כְּמָה שֶׁנֶּאֱמַר: רְבָבָה כְּצֶמַח הַשָּׂדֶה נְתַתִּיךְ, וַתִּרְבִּי וַתִּגְדְּלִי וַתָּבֹאִי בַּעֲדִי עֲדָיִים, שָׁדַיִם נָכֹנוּ וּשְׂעָרֵךְ צִמֵּחַ, וְאַתְּ עֵרֹם וְעֶרְיָה. וָאֶעֱבֹר עָלַיִךְ וָאֶרְאֵךְ מִתְבּוֹסֶסֶת בְּדָמָיִךְ, וָאֹמַר לָךְ בְּדָמַיִךְ חֲיִי, וָאֹמַר לָךְ בְּדָמַיִךְ חֲיִי.

"AS a small number" – as it is stated, "With seventy souls did your ancestors come down to Egypt, and now the Lord your God has made you as numerous as the stars of the sky" (Deuteronomy 10:22).

"AND he became there a nation" – this teaches that Israel became a distinct group there.

"GREAT, powerful" – as it is stated, "The Children of Israel multiplied and increased and grew numerous and very strong, and the land became full of them" (Exodus 1:7).

"AND numerous" – as it is stated, "I have made you numerous as the vegetation of the field, and you increased and grew and were adorned. Your breasts were formed and your hair was long, but you were naked and barren" (Ezekiel 16:7).

וַיָּרֵעוּ אֹתָנוּ הַמִּצְרִים וַיְעַנּוּנוּ, וַיִּתְּנוּ עָלֵינוּ עֲבֹדָה קָשָׁה.

"THE Egyptians treated us badly, and afflicted us, and put upon us hard work" (Deuteronomy 26:6).

"וַיָּרֵעוּ אֹתָנוּ הַמִּצְרִים" – כְּמָה שֶׁנֶּאֱמַר: הָבָה נִתְחַכְּמָה לוֹ פֶּן יִרְבֶּה, וְהָיָה כִּי תִקְרֶאנָה מִלְחָמָה וְנוֹסַף גַּם הוּא עַל שֹׂנְאֵינוּ וְנִלְחַם־בָּנוּ, וְעָלָה מִן־הָאָרֶץ.

"וַיְעַנּוּנוּ" – כְּמָה שֶׁנֶּאֱמַר: וַיָּשִׂימוּ עָלָיו שָׂרֵי מִסִּים לְמַעַן עַנֹּתוֹ בְּסִבְלֹתָם. וַיִּבֶן עָרֵי מִסְכְּנוֹת לְפַרְעֹה. אֶת־פִּתֹם וְאֶת־רַעַמְסֵס.

"וַיִּתְּנוּ עָלֵינוּ עֲבֹדָה קָשָׁה" – כְּמָה שֶׁנֶּאֱמַר: וַיַּעֲבִדוּ מִצְרַיִם אֶת־בְּנֵי יִשְׂרָאֵל בְּפָרֶךְ.

"THE Egyptians treated us badly" – as it is stated, *"Let us be clever toward them, lest they multiply so that when war is declared, they join with our enemies and fight against us and rise up from the land"* (Exodus 1:10).

"AND afflicted us" – as it is stated, *"They placed over them taskmasters in order to afflict them with their burdens; and they built storage cities for Pharaoh, Pitom and Ra'amses"* (Exodus 1:11).

"AND put upon us hard work" – as it is stated, *"They enslaved the children of Israel with hard work"* (Exodus 1:13).

וַנִּצְעַק אֶל־הֹ׳ אֱלֹהֵי אֲבֹתֵינוּ, וַיִּשְׁמַע הֹ׳ אֶת־קֹלֵנוּ, וַיַּרְא אֶת־עָנְיֵנוּ וְאֶת עֲמָלֵנוּ וְאֶת לַחֲצֵנוּ

*"**WE** cried out to the Lord, the God of our ancestors, and the Lord heard our voice, and He saw our affliction, and our toil, and our duress" (Deuteronomy 26:7).*

"וַנִּצְעַק אֶל־הֹ׳ אֱלֹהֵי אֲבֹתֵינוּ" – כְּמָה שֶׁנֶּאֱמַר: וַיְהִי בַיָּמִים הָרַבִּים הָהֵם וַיָּמָת מֶלֶךְ מִצְרַיִם, וַיֵּאָנְחוּ בְנֵי־יִשְׂרָאֵל מִן־הָעֲבוֹדָה וַיִּזְעָקוּ, וַתַּעַל שַׁוְעָתָם אֶל־הָאֱלֹהִים מִן הָעֲבֹדָה.

"וַיִּשְׁמַע הֹ׳ אֶת קֹלֵנוּ" – כְּמָה שֶׁנֶּאֱמַר: וַיִּשְׁמַע אֱלֹהִים אֶת־נַאֲקָתָם, וַיִּזְכֹּר אֱלֹהִים אֶת־בְּרִיתוֹ אֶת־אַבְרָהָם, אֶת־יִצְחָק וְאֶת־יַעֲקֹב.

"וַיַּרְא אֶת־עָנְיֵנוּ" – זוֹ פְּרִישׁוּת דֶּרֶךְ אֶרֶץ, כְּמָה שֶׁנֶּאֱמַר: וַיַּרְא אֱלֹהִים אֶת בְּנֵי־יִשְׂרָאֵל וַיֵּדַע אֱלֹהִים.

"וְאֶת־עֲמָלֵנוּ" – אֵלּוּ הַבָּנִים. כְּמָה שֶׁנֶּאֱמַר: כָּל־הַבֵּן הַיִּלּוֹד הַיְאֹרָה תַּשְׁלִיכֻהוּ וְכָל־הַבַּת תְּחַיּוּן.

"וְאֶת לַחֲצֵנוּ" – זֶה הַדְּחַק, כְּמָה שֶׁנֶּאֱמַר: וְגַם־רָאִיתִי אֶת־הַלַּחַץ אֲשֶׁר מִצְרַיִם לֹחֲצִים אֹתָם.

*"**WE** cried out to the Lord, the God of our ancestors" – as it is stated, "And it happened over the course of time that the king of Egypt died. And the Children of Israel groaned from their work and cried out, and the supplication went up to God from their slavery" (Exodus 2:23).*

*"**AND** the Lord heard our voice" – as it is stated, "And God heard their groans, and God remembered His covenant with Avraham and with Yitzchak and with Ya'akov" (Exodus 2:24).*

*"**AND** He saw our affliction" – this refers to family separation, as it is stated, "And God saw the Children of Israel, and God knew" (Exodus 2:25).*

*"**AND** our toil" – this refers to the killing of the sons, as it is stated, "Every boy that is born, you should throw into the Nile; and every girl, you shall keep alive" (Exodus 1:22).*

*"**AND** our duress" – this refers to the pressure, as it is stated, "And I saw the duress that the Egyptians placed on them" (Exodus 3:9).*

וַיּוֹצִאֵנוּ ה' מִמִּצְרַיִם בְּיָד חֲזָקָה, וּבִזְרֹעַ נְטוּיָה, וּבְמֹרָא גָּדֹל, וּבְאֹתוֹת וּבְמֹפְתִים.

"THE Lord took us out of Egypt with a strong hand and with an outstretched arm and with great awe, and with signs, and with wonders" (Deuteronomy 26:8).

"וַיּוֹצִאֵנוּ ה' מִמִּצְרַיִם" – לֹא עַל־יְדֵי מַלְאָךְ, וְלֹא עַל־יְדֵי שָׂרָף, וְלֹא עַל־יְדֵי שָׁלִיחַ, אֶלָּא הַקָּדוֹשׁ בָּרוּךְ הוּא בִּכְבוֹדוֹ וּבְעַצְמוֹ. שֶׁנֶּאֱמַר: וְעָבַרְתִּי בְאֶרֶץ מִצְרַיִם בַּלַּיְלָה הַזֶּה, וְהִכֵּיתִי כָל־בְּכוֹר בְּאֶרֶץ מִצְרַיִם מֵאָדָם וְעַד בְּהֵמָה, וּבְכָל אֱלֹהֵי מִצְרַיִם אֶעֱשֶׂה שְׁפָטִים. אֲנִי ה'. וְעָבַרְתִּי בְאֶרֶץ מִצְרַיִם בַּלַּיְלָה הַזֶּה – אֲנִי וְלֹא מַלְאָךְ; וְהִכֵּיתִי כָל בְּכוֹר בְּאֶרֶץ־מִצְרַיִם – אֲנִי וְלֹא שָׂרָף; וּבְכָל־אֱלֹהֵי מִצְרַיִם אֶעֱשֶׂה שְׁפָטִים – אֲנִי וְלֹא הַשָּׁלִיחַ; אֲנִי ה' – אֲנִי הוּא וְלֹא אַחֵר.

"בְּיָד חֲזָקָה" – זוֹ הַדֶּבֶר, כְּמָה שֶׁנֶּאֱמַר: הִנֵּה יַד־ה' הוֹיָה בְּמִקְנְךָ אֲשֶׁר בַּשָּׂדֶה, בַּסּוּסִים, בַּחֲמֹרִים, בַּגְּמַלִּים, בַּבָּקָר וּבַצֹּאן, דֶּבֶר כָּבֵד מְאֹד.

"וּבִזְרֹעַ נְטוּיָה" – זוֹ הַחֶרֶב, כְּמָה שֶׁנֶּאֱמַר: וְחַרְבּוֹ שְׁלוּפָה בְּיָדוֹ, נְטוּיָה עַל־יְרוּשָׁלָיִם.

"וּבְמוֹרָא גָּדֹל" – זוֹ גִּלּוּי שְׁכִינָה. כְּמָה שֶׁנֶּאֱמַר, אוֹ הֲנִסָּה אֱלֹהִים לָבוֹא לָקַחַת לוֹ גוֹי מִקֶּרֶב גּוֹי בְּמַסֹּת בְּאֹתֹת וּבְמוֹפְתִים וּבְמִלְחָמָה וּבְיָד חֲזָקָה וּבִזְרוֹעַ נְטוּיָה וּבְמוֹרָאִים גְּדוֹלִים כְּכֹל אֲשֶׁר־עָשָׂה לָכֶם ה' אֱלֹהֵיכֶם בְּמִצְרַיִם לְעֵינֶיךָ.

"וּבְאֹתוֹת" – זֶה הַמַּטֶּה, כְּמָה שֶׁנֶּאֱמַר: וְאֶת הַמַּטֶּה הַזֶּה תִּקַּח בְּיָדֶךָ, אֲשֶׁר תַּעֲשֶׂה־בּוֹ אֶת הָאֹתוֹת.

"וּבְמֹפְתִים" – זֶה הַדָּם, כְּמָה שֶׁנֶּאֱמַר: וְנָתַתִּי מוֹפְתִים בַּשָּׁמַיִם וּבָאָרֶץ.

"THE Lord took us out of Egypt" – not through an angel and not through a seraph and not through a messenger, but by the Holy One, blessed be He, Himself, as it is stated, "I will pass through the Land of Egypt on that night and I will smite every firstborn in the Land of Egypt, from men to animals; and for all the gods of Egypt I will make judgments. I am the Lord" (Exodus 12:12). "I will pass through the Land of Egypt" – I and not an angel. "And I will smite every firstborn" – I and not a seraph. "And with all the gods of Egypt I will make judgments" – I and not a messenger. "I am the Lord" – I am He and there is no other.

"**WITH** a strong hand" – this refers to the pestilence, as it is stated, "Behold the hand of the Lord is upon your herds that are in the field, upon the horses, upon the donkeys, upon the camels, upon the cattle, and upon the flocks – a very heavy pestilence" (Exodus 9:3).

"**AND** with an outstretched arm" – this refers to the sword, as it is stated, "And his sword was drawn in his hand, outstretched over Jerusalem" (I Chronicles 21:16).

"**AND** with great awe" – this refers to the Divine Presence, as it is stated, "Has any god tried to take one nation out from among another nation, with trials, with signs and wonders, and with war and a strong hand and an outstretched arm, and with great and awesome acts, like all that the Lord, your God, did for you in Egypt before your eyes?" (Deuteronomy 4:34).

"**AND** with signs" – this refers to the staff, as it is stated, "And this staff you shall take in your hand, that with it you will perform signs" (Exodus 4:17).

"**AND** with wonders" – this refers to the blood, as it is stated, "I will place my wonders in the skies and in the earth":

Oil Pressers,
Alibag, India,
2001

A Mighty Hand and an Outstretched Arm

This biblical phrase is actually Egyptian in origin: inscriptions from the Egyptian New Kingdom (1500–1200 BCE) – the period of the enslavement in Egypt – routinely describe the pharaoh as "the mighty hand," and his acts (whether on the battlefield or in hunting expeditions) as those of "the outstretched arm."

Why would the Torah describe God in the same terms used by the Egyptians to exalt their pharaoh? We see here the dynamics of cultural appropriation. During much of its history, ancient Israel was in Egypt's shadow. For weak and oppressed peoples, one form of cultural and spiritual resistance is to appropriate the symbols of the oppressor for competitive ideological purposes.

– Rabbi Dr. Joshua Berman

Summer Camp, Tumwater, Washington, USA, 2002

כשאומר דם ואש ותימרות עשן, עשר המכות ודצ״ך עד״ש באח״ב – ישפוך מן הכוס מעט יין:

When you say, "blood and fire and pillars of smoke," the ten plagues, and "*detzach, adash, b'achav*," pour out a little wine from your cup.

דָּם וָאֵשׁ וְתִימְרוֹת עָשָׁן.

"*BLOOD* and fire and pillars of smoke" (Joel 3:3).

דָּבָר אַחֵר: בְּיָד חֲזָקָה – שְׁתַּיִם, וּבִזְרֹעַ נְטוּיָה – שְׁתַּיִם, וּבְמֹרָא גָּדֹל – שְׁתַּיִם, וּבְאֹתוֹת – שְׁתַּיִם, וּבְמֹפְתִים – שְׁתַּיִם.

ANOTHER explanation: "*With a strong hand*" is two plagues; "*and with an outstretched forearm*" is two; "*and with great awe*," two; "*and with signs*," two; "*and with wonders*," two.

Left: *Outdoor Market*,
Samarkand, Uzbekistan, 1998

עשר המכות
Aseret Hamakkot: The Ten Plagues

אֵלּוּ עֶשֶׂר מַכּוֹת שֶׁהֵבִיא הַקָּדוֹשׁ בָּרוּךְ הוּא עַל־הַמִּצְרִים בְּמִצְרַיִם, וְאֵלּוּ הֵן:

THESE *are the ten plagues that the Holy One, blessed be He, brought on the Egyptians in Egypt, and they are as follows:*

BLOOD	דָּם
FROGS	צְפַרְדֵּעַ
LICE	כִּנִּים
WILD ANIMALS	עָרוֹב
PESTILENCE	דֶּבֶר
BOILS	שְׁחִין
HAIL	בָּרָד
LOCUSTS	אַרְבֶּה
DARKNESS	חֹשֶׁךְ
SLAYING OF THE FIRSTBORN	מַכַּת בְּכוֹרוֹת

רַבִּי יְהוּדָה הָיָה נוֹתֵן בָּהֶם סִמָּנִים: דְּצַ"ךְ עַדַ"שׁ בְּאַחַ"ב.

RABBI *Yehuda offered a mnemonic for them:*
Detzach [the Hebrew initials of the first three plagues], Adash [the second three plagues],
B'achav [the last four].

רַבִּי יוֹסֵי הַגְּלִילִי אוֹמֵר: מִנַּיִן אַתָּה אוֹמֵר שֶׁלָּקוּ הַמִּצְרִים בְּמִצְרַיִם עֶשֶׂר מַכּוֹת וְעַל הַיָּם לָקוּ חֲמִשִּׁים מַכּוֹת? בְּמִצְרַיִם מַה הוּא אוֹמֵר? וַיֹּאמְרוּ הַחַרְטֻמִּם אֶל פַּרְעֹה: אֶצְבַּע אֱלֹהִים הִוא, וְעַל הַיָּם מָה הוּא אוֹמֵר? וַיַּרְא יִשְׂרָאֵל אֶת־הַיָּד הַגְּדֹלָה אֲשֶׁר עָשָׂה ה' בְּמִצְרַיִם, וַיִּירְאוּ הָעָם אֶת־ה', וַיַּאֲמִינוּ בַּה' וּבְמֹשֶׁה עַבְדּוֹ. כַּמָּה לָקוּ בְאֶצְבַּע? עֶשֶׂר מַכּוֹת. אֱמֹר מֵעַתָּה: בְּמִצְרַיִם לָקוּ עֶשֶׂר מַכּוֹת וְעַל הַיָּם לָקוּ חֲמִשִּׁים מַכּוֹת.

רַבִּי אֱלִיעֶזֶר אוֹמֵר: מִנַּיִן שֶׁכָּל־מַכָּה וּמַכָּה שֶׁהֵבִיא הַקָּדוֹשׁ בָּרוּךְ הוּא עַל הַמִּצְרִים בְּמִצְרַיִם הָיְתָה שֶׁל אַרְבַּע מַכּוֹת? שֶׁנֶּאֱמַר: יְשַׁלַּח־בָּם חֲרוֹן אַפּוֹ, עֶבְרָה וָזַעַם וְצָרָה, מִשְׁלַחַת מַלְאֲכֵי רָעִים. עֶבְרָה – אַחַת, וָזַעַם – שְׁתַּיִם, וְצָרָה – שָׁלֹשׁ, מִשְׁלַחַת מַלְאֲכֵי רָעִים – אַרְבַּע. אֱמֹר מֵעַתָּה: בְּמִצְרַיִם לָקוּ אַרְבָּעִים מַכּוֹת וְעַל הַיָּם לָקוּ מָאתַיִם מַכּוֹת.

רַבִּי עֲקִיבָא אוֹמֵר: מִנַּיִן שֶׁכָּל־מַכָּה וּמַכָּה שֶׁהֵבִיא הַקָּדוֹשׁ בָּרוּךְ הוּא עַל הַמִּצְרִים בְּמִצְרַיִם הָיְתָה שֶׁל חָמֵשׁ מַכּוֹת? שֶׁנֶּאֱמַר: יְשַׁלַּח־בָּם חֲרוֹן אַפּוֹ, עֶבְרָה וָזַעַם וְצָרָה, מִשְׁלַחַת מַלְאֲכֵי רָעִים. חֲרוֹן אַפּוֹ – אַחַת, עֶבְרָה – שְׁתַּיִם, וָזַעַם – שָׁלֹשׁ, וְצָרָה – אַרְבַּע, מִשְׁלַחַת מַלְאֲכֵי רָעִים – חָמֵשׁ. אֱמֹר מֵעַתָּה: בְּמִצְרַיִם לָקוּ חֲמִשִּׁים מַכּוֹת וְעַל הַיָּם לָקוּ חֲמִשִּׁים וּמָאתַיִם מַכּוֹת.

RABBI *Yose Haglili says: From where can you derive that the Egyptians were struck with ten plagues in Egypt and struck with fifty plagues at the Sea? In Egypt, what does it state? "Then the magicians said unto Pharaoh: 'This is the finger of God'" (Exodus 8:15). And at the Sea, what does it state? "Israel saw the Lord's great hand that He used upon the Egyptians, and the people feared the Lord; and they believed in the Lord, and in Moshe, His servant" (Exodus 14:31). How many were they struck with by the finger? Ten plagues. You can say from here that in Egypt they were struck with ten plagues, and at the Sea they were struck with fifty plagues.*

RABBI Eliezer says: From where can you derive that every plague that the Holy One, blessed be He, brought upon the Egyptians in Egypt was really four plagues? As it is stated, "He sent upon them the fierceness of His anger: wrath, fury, trouble, and messengers of evil" (Psalms 78:49). "Wrath" is one; "fury" is two; "trouble," three; "messengers of evil," four. You can say from here that in Egypt they were struck with forty plagues, and at the Sea they were struck with two hundred plagues.

RABBI Akiva says: From where can you derive that every plague that the Holy One, blessed be He, brought upon the Egyptians in Egypt was really five plagues? As it is stated, "He sent upon them the fierceness of His anger, wrath, fury, trouble, and messengers of evil" (Psalms 78:49). "The fierceness of His anger" is one; "wrath," two; "fury," three; "trouble," four; "messengers of evil," five. You can say from here that in Egypt they were struck with fifty plagues, and at the Sea they were struck with two hundred fifty plagues.

Left: *Palmachim Beach,*
Israel, 2002

דַּיֵּנוּ
Dayenu

כַּמָּה מַעֲלוֹת טוֹבוֹת לַמָּקוֹם עָלֵינוּ!

אִלּוּ הוֹצִיאָנוּ מִמִּצְרַיִם וְלֹא עָשָׂה בָהֶם שְׁפָטִים, דַּיֵּנוּ.

אִלּוּ עָשָׂה בָהֶם שְׁפָטִים, וְלֹא עָשָׂה בֵאלֹהֵיהֶם, דַּיֵּנוּ.

אִלּוּ עָשָׂה בֵאלֹהֵיהֶם, וְלֹא הָרַג אֶת־בְּכוֹרֵיהֶם, דַּיֵּנוּ.

אִלּוּ הָרַג אֶת־בְּכוֹרֵיהֶם וְלֹא נָתַן לָנוּ אֶת־מָמוֹנָם, דַּיֵּנוּ.

אִלּוּ נָתַן לָנוּ אֶת־מָמוֹנָם וְלֹא קָרַע לָנוּ אֶת־הַיָּם, דַּיֵּנוּ.

אִלּוּ קָרַע לָנוּ אֶת־הַיָּם וְלֹא הֶעֱבִירָנוּ בְּתוֹכוֹ בֶּחָרָבָה, דַּיֵּנוּ.

אִלּוּ הֶעֱבִירָנוּ בְּתוֹכוֹ בֶּחָרָבָה וְלֹא שִׁקַּע צָרֵינוּ בְּתוֹכוֹ, דַּיֵּנוּ.

אִלּוּ שִׁקַּע צָרֵינוּ בְּתוֹכוֹ וְלֹא סִפֵּק צָרְכֵּנוּ בַּמִּדְבָּר אַרְבָּעִים שָׁנָה, דַּיֵּנוּ.

אִלּוּ סִפֵּק צָרְכֵּנוּ בְּמִדְבָּר אַרְבָּעִים שָׁנָה וְלֹא הֶאֱכִילָנוּ אֶת־הַמָּן, דַּיֵּנוּ.

אִלּוּ הֶאֱכִילָנוּ אֶת־הַמָּן וְלֹא נָתַן לָנוּ אֶת־הַשַּׁבָּת, דַּיֵּנוּ.

אִלּוּ נָתַן לָנוּ אֶת־הַשַּׁבָּת, וְלֹא קֵרְבָנוּ לִפְנֵי הַר סִינַי, דַּיֵּנוּ.

אִלּוּ קֵרְבָנוּ לִפְנֵי הַר סִינַי, וְלֹא נַתַן לָנוּ אֶת־הַתּוֹרָה, דַּיֵּנוּ.

אִלּוּ נַתַן לָנוּ אֶת־הַתּוֹרָה וְלֹא הִכְנִיסָנוּ לְאֶרֶץ יִשְׂרָאֵל, דַּיֵּנוּ.

אִלּוּ הִכְנִיסָנוּ לְאֶרֶץ יִשְׂרָאֵל וְלֹא בָנָה לָנוּ אֶת־בֵּית הַבְּחִירָה, דַּיֵּנוּ.

 Scan here to hear a popular tune for the song "Dayenu."

HOW *many degrees of good did the Eternal One bestow upon us!*

IF *He had taken us out of Egypt and not made judgments on them, it would have been enough for us.*

IF *He had made judgments on them and not on their gods, it would have been enough for us.*

IF *He had made judgments on their gods and not killed their firstborn, it would have been enough for us.*

IF *He had killed their firstborn and not given us their money, it would have been enough for us.*

IF *He had given us their money and not split the Sea for us, it would have been enough for us.*

IF *He had split the Sea for us and had not taken us through it on dry land, it would have been enough for us.*

IF *He had taken us through it on dry land and not drowned our enemies in the Sea, it would have been enough for us.*

IF *He had drowned our enemies and not taken care of our needs in the wilderness for forty years, it would have been enough for us.*

IF *He had taken care of our needs in the wilderness for forty years and not fed us the manna, it would have been enough for us.*

IF *He had fed us the manna and not given us the Shabbat, it would have been enough for us.*

IF *He had given us the Shabbat and not brought us close to Mount Sinai, it would have been enough for us.*

IF *He had brought us close to Mount Sinai and not given us the Torah, it would have been enough for us.*

IF *He had given us the Torah and not brought us into the land of Israel, it would have been enough for us.*

IF *He had brought us into the land of Israel and not built us the "Chosen House" [the Temple], it would have been enough for us.*

עַל אַחַת, כַּמָּה וְכַמָּה, טוֹבָה כְּפוּלָה וּמְכֻפֶּלֶת לַמָּקוֹם עָלֵינוּ: שֶׁהוֹצִיאָנוּ מִמִּצְרַיִם, וְעָשָׂה בָהֶם שְׁפָטִים, וְעָשָׂה בֵאלֹהֵיהֶם, וְהָרַג אֶת־בְּכוֹרֵיהֶם, וְנָתַן לָנוּ אֶת־מָמוֹנָם, וְקָרַע לָנוּ אֶת־הַיָּם, וְהֶעֱבִירָנוּ בְּתוֹכוֹ בֶּחָרָבָה, וְשִׁקַּע צָרֵינוּ בְּתוֹכוֹ, וְסִפֵּק צָרְכֵּנוּ בַּמִּדְבָּר אַרְבָּעִים שָׁנָה, וְהֶאֱכִילָנוּ אֶת־הַמָּן, וְנָתַן לָנוּ אֶת־הַשַּׁבָּת, וְקֵרְבָנוּ לִפְנֵי הַר סִינַי, וְנָתַן לָנוּ אֶת־הַתּוֹרָה, וְהִכְנִיסָנוּ לְאֶרֶץ יִשְׂרָאֵל, וּבָנָה לָנוּ אֶת־בֵּית הַבְּחִירָה לְכַפֵּר עַל־כָּל־עֲוֹנוֹתֵינוּ.

HOW much more is the good doubled and quadrupled that the Eternal One bestowed upon us? For He took us out of Egypt, and made judgments upon them, and made judgments upon their gods, and killed their firstborn, and gave us their money, and split the Sea for us, and brought us through it on dry land, and drowned our enemies, and took care of our needs in the wilderness for forty years, and fed us the manna, and gave us the Shabbat, and brought us close to Mount Sinai, and gave us the Torah, and brought us into the land of Israel, and built for us the "Chosen House" [the Temple] to atone for all our sins.

Jewish Quarter,
Jerusalem, Israel,
1984

פסח מצה ומרור
Pesach, Matzah u'Maror:
Passover, Matzah, and Maror

רַבָּן גַּמְלִיאֵל הָיָה אוֹמֵר: כָּל שֶׁלֹּא אָמַר שְׁלֹשָׁה דְבָרִים אֵלּוּ בַּפֶּסַח, לֹא יָצָא יְדֵי חוֹבָתוֹ, וְאֵלּוּ הֵן: פֶּסַח, מַצָּה, וּמָרוֹר.

פֶּסַח שֶׁהָיוּ אֲבוֹתֵינוּ אוֹכְלִים בִּזְמַן שֶׁבֵּית הַמִּקְדָּשׁ הָיָה קַיָּם, עַל שׁוּם מָה? עַל שׁוּם שֶׁפָּסַח הַקָּדוֹשׁ בָּרוּךְ הוּא עַל בָּתֵּי אֲבוֹתֵינוּ בְּמִצְרַיִם, שֶׁנֶּאֱמַר: וַאֲמַרְתֶּם זֶבַח פֶּסַח הוּא לַה', אֲשֶׁר פָּסַח עַל בָּתֵּי בְנֵי יִשְׂרָאֵל בְּמִצְרַיִם בְּנָגְפּוֹ אֶת־מִצְרַיִם, וְאֶת־בָּתֵּינוּ הִצִּיל וַיִּקֹּד הָעָם וַיִּשְׁתַּחֲווּ.

אוֹחֵז הַמַּצָּה בְּיָדוֹ וּמַרְאֶה אוֹתָהּ לַמְסֻבִּים:

מַצָּה זוֹ שֶׁאָנוּ אוֹכְלִים, עַל שׁוּם מָה? עַל שׁוּם שֶׁלֹּא הִסְפִּיק בְּצֵקָם שֶׁל אֲבוֹתֵינוּ לְהַחֲמִיץ עַד שֶׁנִּגְלָה עֲלֵיהֶם מֶלֶךְ מַלְכֵי הַמְּלָכִים, הַקָּדוֹשׁ בָּרוּךְ הוּא, וּגְאָלָם, שֶׁנֶּאֱמַר: וַיֹּאפוּ אֶת־הַבָּצֵק אֲשֶׁר הוֹצִיאוּ מִמִּצְרַיִם עֻגֹת מַצּוֹת, כִּי לֹא חָמֵץ, כִּי גֹרְשׁוּ מִמִּצְרַיִם וְלֹא יָכְלוּ לְהִתְמַהְמֵהַּ, וְגַם צֵדָה לֹא עָשׂוּ לָהֶם.

אוֹחֵז הַמָּרוֹר בְּיָדוֹ וּמַרְאֶה אוֹתוֹ לַמְסֻבִּים:

מָרוֹר זֶה שֶׁאָנוּ אוֹכְלִים, עַל שׁוּם מָה? עַל שׁוּם שֶׁמֵּרְרוּ הַמִּצְרִים אֶת־חַיֵּי אֲבוֹתֵינוּ בְּמִצְרָיִם, שֶׁנֶּאֱמַר: וַיְמָרְרוּ אֶת חַיֵּיהֶם בַּעֲבֹדָה קָשָׁה, בְּחֹמֶר וּבִלְבֵנִים וּבְכָל־עֲבֹדָה בַּשָּׂדֶה אֵת כָּל עֲבֹדָתָם אֲשֶׁר עָבְדוּ בָהֶם בְּפָרֶךְ.

RABBAN Gamliel used to say, "Anyone who has not mentioned these three items on Pesach has not fulfilled his obligation, and these are they: the Pesach sacrifice, matzah, and maror."

THE Pesach sacrifice that our ancestors used to eat when the Temple existed – what is it for? It was because the Holy One, blessed be He, passed over the homes of our ancestors in Egypt, as it is stated, "You shall say, 'It is a Passover sacrifice to the Lord, who passed over the homes of the Children of Israel in Egypt when He smote the Egyptians. And He saved our homes, and the people bowed their heads and prayed'" (Exodus 12:27).

Hold the matzah and show it to the others.

THIS matzah that we eat – what is it for? It is for our ancestors' dough that was not able to rise before the King of kings, the Holy One, blessed be He, revealed Himself to them and redeemed them, as it is stated, "And they baked the dough that they brought out of Egypt into matzah cakes, which did not rise; because they were expelled from Egypt and could not delay, they had not made provisions for themselves" (Exodus 12:39).

Hold the maror and show it to the others.

THIS maror [bitter herb] that we eat – what is it for? It is because the Egyptians embittered the lives of our ancestors in Egypt, as it is stated, "They made their lives bitter with hard work, in mortar and in brick, and in all manner of work in the field. All the work with which they enslaved them was harsh" (Exodus 1:14).

מַצָּה זו שֶׁאָנוּ אוֹכְלִים
"This matzah that we eat..."

Matzah Oven, Bukhara, Uzbekistan, 2000

What attitude toward matzah is conveyed in this photograph? How does it connect with your own feelings about matzah?

Do we lose out on something when we eat matzah from a box and don't bake it ourselves?

How might the Seder experience feel different if we could say "this matzah that we bake" and not just "this matzah that we eat"?

Scan here for further questions and texts relating to this photograph.

62

בְּכָל־דּוֹר וָדוֹר

B'chol Dor va'Dor:
In Each and Every Generation

בְּכָל־דּוֹר וָדוֹר חַיָּב אָדָם לִרְאוֹת [סְפָרַדִּים אוֹמְרִים: "לְהַרְאוֹת"] אֶת־עַצְמוֹ כְּאִלּוּ הוּא יָצָא מִמִּצְרַיִם, שֶׁנֶּאֱמַר: וְהִגַּדְתָּ לְבִנְךָ בַּיּוֹם הַהוּא לֵאמֹר, בַּעֲבוּר זֶה עָשָׂה ה' לִי בְּצֵאתִי מִמִּצְרָיִם. לֹא אֶת־אֲבוֹתֵינוּ בִּלְבַד גָּאַל הַקָּדוֹשׁ בָּרוּךְ הוּא, אֶלָּא אַף אוֹתָנוּ גָּאַל עִמָּהֶם, שֶׁנֶּאֱמַר: וְאוֹתָנוּ הוֹצִיא מִשָּׁם, לְמַעַן הָבִיא אוֹתָנוּ, לָתֶת לָנוּ אֶת־הָאָרֶץ אֲשֶׁר נִשְׁבַּע לַאֲבוֹתֵינוּ.

IN each and every generation, a person is obligated to see [Sephardim say: "to show"] oneself as if he or she left Egypt, as it is stated, "You shall explain to your child on that day: It is because of what the Lord did for me when I left Egypt" (Exodus 13:8). It was not only our ancestors that the Holy One, blessed be He, redeemed; rather, He redeemed us along with them, as it is stated, "And He took us out from there, in order to bring us in, to give us the land that He promised to our ancestors" (Deuteronomy 6:23).

In Each and Every Generation

Sephardic Haggadot write that in every generation, each person must show oneself (להראות) as if one left Egypt. The requirement to "show" ourselves as slaves departing Egypt inspired the widely observed Sephardic custom of reenacting this story by dressing up. As a kid, I loved wrapping myself in linens and holding makeshift bundles in the form of pillowcases filled with matzot as my siblings and I performed our own exodus at the Seder.

The impetus to show ourselves as slaves – to relive and perform the exodus – symbolizes Passover's memory covenant. As Paulo Freire put it in his insightful *Pedagogy of the Oppressed,* true liberation occurs when human beings cease to think of themselves as objects of history and instead become subjects of history. On Passover, we ceased being the powerless objects of an Egyptian tyranny seemingly as constant as nature, and became subjects of history – realizing that we could change our fate and embark on the long journey toward freedom.

Every Passover we recall and reenact the exodus and thus announce boldly that we remain subjects of history – imbued with the sacred and liberatory knowledge that we can and must partner with God to engage in action within this world in order to transform it.

– Dr. Mijal Bitton

בְּכָל־דּוֹר וָדוֹר

"In each and every generation…"

Backpack, Operation Solomon, Ben Gurion Airport, Israel, 1991

What do you imagine is the story of this photograph?

How do you interpret the relationship between these two figures?

What forms of exodus have you seen or experienced in your lifetime?

Scan here for further questions and texts relating to this photograph.

מִיָּגוֹן לְשִׂמְחָה, וּמֵאֵבֶל לְיוֹם טוֹב

"...from sorrow to joy, from mourning to festival..."

Holocaust Survivor, Buenos Aires, Argentina, 2002

 Why do you think the photographer chose to group this Holocaust survivor with his granddaughters? How can we, or should we, share painful events from our history?

Scan here for further questions and texts relating to this photograph.

חצי הלל
Chatzi Hallel: First Half of Hallel

יאחז הכוס בידו ויכסה המצות ויאמר:

Raise the Kiddush cup, cover the matzah, and say:

לְפִיכָךְ אֲנַחְנוּ חַיָּבִים לְהוֹדוֹת, לְהַלֵּל, לְשַׁבֵּחַ, לְפָאֵר, לְרוֹמֵם, לְהַדֵּר, לְבָרֵךְ, לְעַלֵּה וּלְקַלֵּס לְמִי שֶׁעָשָׂה לַאֲבוֹתֵינוּ וְלָנוּ אֶת־כָּל־הַנִּסִּים הָאֵלּוּ: הוֹצִיאָנוּ מֵעַבְדוּת לְחֵרוּת, מִיָּגוֹן לְשִׂמְחָה, וּמֵאֵבֶל לְיוֹם טוֹב, וּמֵאֲפֵלָה לְאוֹר גָּדוֹל, וּמִשִּׁעְבּוּד לִגְאֻלָּה. וְנֹאמַר לְפָנָיו שִׁירָה חֲדָשָׁה: הַלְלוּיָהּ.

הַלְלוּיָהּ הַלְלוּ עַבְדֵי ה', הַלְלוּ אֶת־שֵׁם ה'. יְהִי שֵׁם ה' מְבֹרָךְ מֵעַתָּה וְעַד עוֹלָם. מִמִּזְרַח שֶׁמֶשׁ עַד מְבוֹאוֹ מְהֻלָּל שֵׁם ה'. רָם עַל־כָּל־גּוֹיִם ה', עַל הַשָּׁמַיִם כְּבוֹדוֹ. מִי כַה' אֱלֹהֵינוּ הַמַּגְבִּיהִי לָשָׁבֶת, הַמַּשְׁפִּילִי לִרְאוֹת בַּשָּׁמַיִם וּבָאָרֶץ? מְקִימִי מֵעָפָר דָּל, מֵאַשְׁפֹּת יָרִים אֶבְיוֹן, לְהוֹשִׁיבִי עִם־נְדִיבִים, עִם נְדִיבֵי עַמּוֹ. מוֹשִׁיבִי עֲקֶרֶת הַבַּיִת, אֵם הַבָּנִים שְׂמֵחָה. הַלְלוּיָהּ.

בְּצֵאת יִשְׂרָאֵל מִמִּצְרַיִם, בֵּית יַעֲקֹב מֵעַם לֹעֵז, הָיְתָה יְהוּדָה לְקָדְשׁוֹ, יִשְׂרָאֵל מַמְשְׁלוֹתָיו. הַיָּם רָאָה וַיָּנֹס, הַיַּרְדֵּן יִסֹּב לְאָחוֹר. הֶהָרִים רָקְדוּ כְאֵילִים, גְּבָעוֹת כִּבְנֵי צֹאן. מַה לְּךָ הַיָּם כִּי תָנוּס, הַיַּרְדֵּן תִּסֹּב לְאָחוֹר, הֶהָרִים תִּרְקְדוּ כְאֵילִים, גְּבָעוֹת כִּבְנֵי־צֹאן. מִלִּפְנֵי אָדוֹן חוּלִי אָרֶץ, מִלִּפְנֵי אֱלוֹהַּ יַעֲקֹב. הַהֹפְכִי הַצּוּר אֲגַם־מָיִם, חַלָּמִישׁ לְמַעְיְנוֹ־מָיִם.

THEREFORE *we are obligated to thank, praise, laud, glorify, exalt, lavish, bless, raise high, and acclaim He who made all these miracles for our ancestors and for us: He brought us out from slavery to freedom, from sorrow to joy, from mourning to festival, from darkness to great light, and from servitude to redemption. And let us recite a new song before Him, Halleluyah!*

HALLELUYAH! *Praise the servants of the Lord, praise the name of the Lord. May the name of the Lord be blessed from now and forever. From the rising of the sun in the East to its setting, the name of the Lord is praised. Above all nations is the Lord, His honor is above the heavens. Who is like the Lord, our God, who sits above, who looks down upon the heavens and the earth? He brings up the poor from the dust; from the refuse He raises the destitute, to seat him with the nobles, with the nobles of his people. He makes the barren woman a happy mother of children. Halleluyah! (Psalms 113)*

67

WHEN *Israel went out from Egypt – the House of Ya'akov from a people of a foreign tongue – Yehudah became His holy one, Israel, His dominion. The sea saw and fled, the Jordan turned back. The mountains danced like rams, the hills like young sheep. What is happening to you, O sea, that you are fleeing, O Jordan that you turn back, O mountains that you dance like rams, O hills like young sheep? From before the Master, tremble O earth, from before the Lord of Ya'akov – He who turns the boulder into a pond of water, the flint into a spring. (Psalms 114)*

 While the Haggadah text remains virtually unchanged throughout the world, diverse communities bring their own customs and melodies to the Seder ritual.

Scan here to hear how different Jewish communities sing Hallel.

הֶהָרִים רָקְדוּ כְאֵילִים, גְּבָעוֹת כִּבְנֵי צֹאן

"*The mountains danced like rams, the hills like young sheep…*"

Amiaz Plains, Israel, 2002

How would you describe the hills and mountains in this photograph?
What do you think the psalmist meant by the phrase "the mountains danced like rams"? Have you ever felt the earth move?

Scan here for further questions and texts relating to this photograph.

כוס שנייה
Kos Shniah: Second Cup of Wine

מגביהים את הכוס עד גאל ישראל.
Raise the Kiddush cup and say:

בָּרוּךְ אַתָּה ה׳ אֱלֹהֵינוּ מֶלֶךְ הָעוֹלָם, אֲשֶׁר גְּאָלָנוּ וְגָאַל אֶת־אֲבוֹתֵינוּ מִמִּצְרַיִם, וְהִגִּיעָנוּ הַלַּיְלָה הַזֶּה לֶאֱכָל־בּוֹ מַצָּה וּמָרוֹר. כֵּן ה׳ אֱלֹהֵינוּ וֵאלֹהֵי אֲבוֹתֵינוּ יַגִּיעֵנוּ לְמוֹעֲדִים וְלִרְגָלִים אֲחֵרִים הַבָּאִים לִקְרָאתֵנוּ לְשָׁלוֹם, שְׂמֵחִים בְּבִנְיַן עִירֶךָ וְשָׂשִׂים בַּעֲבוֹדָתֶךָ. וְנֹאכַל שָׁם מִן הַפְּסָחִים וּמִן הַזְּבָחִים אֲשֶׁר יַגִּיעַ דָּמָם עַל קִיר מִזְבַּחֲךָ לְרָצוֹן, וְנוֹדֶה לְךָ שִׁיר חָדָשׁ עַל גְּאֻלָּתֵנוּ וְעַל פְּדוּת נַפְשֵׁנוּ. בָּרוּךְ אַתָּה ה׳, גָּאַל יִשְׂרָאֵל.

BLESSED are You, Lord our God, Sovereign of the universe, who redeemed us and redeemed our ancestors from Egypt, and brought us on this night to eat matzah and maror. So too, Lord our God, and God of our ancestors, bring us to other holidays and festivals that will greet us in peace, joyful in the building of Your city and happy in Your worship. We shall eat there from the offerings and Pesach sacrifices, the blood of which shall reach the wall of Your altar for Your acceptance. And we shall thank You with a new song for our redemption and the restoration of our souls. Blessed are You, Lord, who redeemed Israel.

שותים את הכוס בהסבת שמאל.
Recite the blessing below and drink the cup while reclining to the left:

בָּרוּךְ אַתָּה ה׳, אֱלֹהֵינוּ מֶלֶךְ הָעוֹלָם בּוֹרֵא פְּרִי הַגָּפֶן.

BLESSED are You, Lord our God, Sovereign of the universe, who creates the fruit of the vine.

Wine Cellar,
Djerba,
Tunisia, 1995

Jewish Community Center, Detroit, USA, 2009

רַחְצָה
RACHTZAH: WASH HANDS

נוטלים את הידיים ומברכים:

Wash hands and recite the following blessing:

בָּרוּךְ אַתָּה ה׳, אֱלֹהֵינוּ מֶלֶךְ הָעוֹלָם, אֲשֶׁר קִדְּשָׁנוּ בְּמִצְוֹתָיו וְצִוָּנוּ עַל נְטִילַת יָדָיִם.

Blessed are You, Lord our God, Sovereign of the universe, who has sanctified us with His commandments and has commanded us to wash the hands.

מוֹצִיא מַצָּה
MOTZI MATZAH: EAT THE MATZAH

יִקַּח הַמַּצוֹת בְּסֵדֶר שֶׁהִנִּיחָן, הַפְּרוּסָה בֵּין שְׁתֵּי הַשְּׁלֵמוֹת, יֹאחֵז שְׁלָשְׁתָּן בְּיָדוֹ
וִיבָרֵךְ ״הַמּוֹצִיא״ בְּכַוָּנָה עַל הָעֶלְיוֹנָה, וְ״עַל אֲכִילַת מַצָּה״ בְּכַוָּנָה עַל הַפְּרוּסָה.
אַחַר כָּךְ יִבְצַע כְּזַיִת מִן הָעֶלְיוֹנָה הַשְּׁלֵמָה וּכְזַיִת שֵׁנִי מִן הַפְּרוּסָה, וְיִטְבְּלֵם בְּמֶלַח, וְיֹאכַל בַּהֲסַבָּה שְׁנֵי הַזֵּיתִים:

Remove the matzot and recite the blessings below.
Break off a piece from the top matzah and another piece from the broken matzah and dip them in salt. Eat them while reclining.

בָּרוּךְ אַתָּה ה׳, אֱלֹהֵינוּ מֶלֶךְ הָעוֹלָם הַמּוֹצִיא לֶחֶם מִן הָאָרֶץ.

Blessed are You, Lord our God, Sovereign of the universe, who brings forth bread from the earth.

בָּרוּךְ אַתָּה ה׳, אֱלֹהֵינוּ מֶלֶךְ הָעוֹלָם, אֲשֶׁר קִדְּשָׁנוּ בְּמִצְוֹתָיו וְצִוָּנוּ עַל אֲכִילַת מַצָּה.

Blessed are You, Lord our God, Sovereign of the universe, who has sanctified us with His commandments and has commanded us to eat matzah.

Letting Go

Passover has always meant for me an opportunity to ask myself, "What has kept me 'enslaved' this year? To what am I beholden?" The exodus from Egypt, in modern times, is really a metaphor for calling on our spirit of resiliency, determination, and what it means to be "free."

We get very comfortable and complacent in our everyday lives, and sometimes we need a reason to take a step back, to assess our commitments, relationships, and way of being and really ask ourselves, "Am I free?" And, if the answer is no, then "What do I need to let go of to be free?" That can be something tangible or it can be an emotion – such as anger or resentment. Passover bookends the year for reflection (with Yom Kippur and Rosh Hashanah being the other bookend). And I always look forward to thinking of things about which I can say "Let it go."

– **Karma Lowe**

מָרוֹר
MAROR: EAT THE MAROR

כל אחד מהמסבים לוקח כזית מרור, מטבלו בחרוסת, מנער החרוסת, מברך ואוכל בלי הסבה.

Everyone should take a piece of maror, dip it into the charoset, make the blessing, and eat it without reclining.

בָּרוּךְ אַתָּה ה׳, אֱלֹהֵינוּ מֶלֶךְ הָעוֹלָם, אֲשֶׁר קִדְּשָׁנוּ בְּמִצְוֹתָיו וְצִוָּנוּ עַל אֲכִילַת מָרוֹר.

BLESSED are You, Lord our God, Sovereign of the universe, who has sanctified us with His commandments and has commanded us to eat maror.

כּוֹרֵךְ
KORECH: MAKE A SANDWICH

כל אחד מהמסבים לוקח כזית מן המצה השלישית עם כזית מרור, כורכים יחד, אוכלים בהסבה ובלי ברכה. לפני אכלו אומר.

All present should take a piece of matzah with a piece of maror and combine them together.
Recite the following words; then eat the matzah and maror while reclining and without saying a blessing.

זֵכֶר לַמִּקְדָּשׁ כְּהַלֵּל. כֵּן עָשָׂה הַלֵּל בִּזְמַן שֶׁבֵּית הַמִּקְדָּשׁ הָיָה קַיָּם: הָיָה כּוֹרֵךְ מַצָּה וּמָרוֹר וְאוֹכֵל בְּיַחַד, לְקַיֵּם מַה שֶׁנֶּאֱמַר: עַל מַצּוֹת וּמְרוֹרִים יֹאכְלֻהוּ.

IN memory of the Temple, we do as Hillel did. This is what Hillel would do when the Temple existed: He would combine the matzah and maror and eat them together, in order to fulfill what is stated, "Upon matzah and maror you shall eat it" (Exodus 12:8).

Charoset: Harshness and Hope

The mitzvah of eating charoset often gets overlooked during the Pesach Seder. It gets folded in with Korech, Hillel's sandwich, eaten together with matzah and maror. There is no moment to point to it or discuss its meaning. Yet the Talmud in *Pesachim* 116a suggests that eating charoset is required, either as commemoration of the apple tree "where the Israelite women gave birth to their children," or to commemorate the hard labor of Jewish slaves being forced to make bricks.

This one dish captures the duality of Pesach that we reflect throughout the Seder – remembering slavery and hoping for freedom. The apples in the charoset are a symbol of the hope that the Israelite women held onto by continuing to procreate in spite of the devastating darkness that the people faced in Egypt. Every baby brought renewed hope for a better life. The nuts in the charoset, however, are a symbol of the mortar and bricks, commemorating the harshness of their world.

Harshness and hope are the two realities that we must hold in tension with each other. By eating the charoset, we are remembering the harshness of slavery but at the same time committing to restore equilibrium and tranquility to our lives. To never give up hope that out of suffering, new life can emerge, and bitterness can turn into sweetness.

– Rabba Sara Hurwitz

Sunset, Nahariya, Israel, 1995

שֻׁלְחָן עוֹרֵךְ
"The table is set."

Setting the Table, Santiago de Cuba, Cuba, 2003

What attitude toward food does this photograph express? How is it reflected?
How would you describe your own attitudes toward food? Why is food so central
to our social, communal, and religious lives – and such a crucial part of the Seder?
Scan here for further questions and texts relating to this photograph.

שֻׁלְחָן עוֹרֵךְ
SHULCHAN ORECH: ENJOY THE MEAL

אוֹכְלִים וְשׁוֹתִים.
We eat and drink.

New Immigrant,
Lod, Israel, 1997

צָפוּן
TZAFUN: REVEAL THE HIDDEN MATZAH

אחר גמר הסעודה לוקח כל אחד מהמסובים כזית מהמצה שהייתה צפונה לאפיקומן
ואוכל ממנה כזית בהסבה. וצריך לאוכלה קודם חצות הלילה.

After the meal, all those present take a piece from the matzah that was hidden, recite the following, and eat the matzah while reclining.

זֵכֶר לְקָרְבַּן פֶּסַח הַנֶּאֱכָל עַל הַשֹּׂבַע.

This is in memory of the Pesach sacrifice that was eaten upon being satiated.

A Passover Memory

We were five kids in a tiny apartment in Montreal. Even as spring beckoned, the cold tremors of winter were still out there. Inside, we felt the bustling anticipation of the first Seder. The aromas of my mother's cooking reached every corner of the apartment. An extended table was set up in the hallway to accommodate a few guests.

Everything on the table felt new – the china, the tablecloth, the glasses, the silverware, the colors. Our clothes were also new. Perhaps as a nod to nostalgia, my parents would wear colorful *jalabas*. Of course, they could never recreate the open-air, Mediterranean atmosphere of Passover in their cozy and noisy Jewish neighborhood of Casablanca. But for one night at least, they turned an isolated apartment in frigid Montreal into a glorious and intimate sanctuary that their son would write about a half century later.

– **David Suissa**

וְאָכַלְתָּ וְשָׂבַעְתָּ וּבֵרַכְתָּ

"You shall eat and you shall be satisfied and you shall bless..."

Grace after Meal, Jewish Day School, Casablanca, Morocco, 2004

 How would you describe the expression on this boy's face?

Why do you think we wait until we're satisfied to offer thanks for our meal?

Scan here for further questions and texts relating to this photograph.

81

בָּרֵךְ
BARECH: BLESS AFTER THE MEAL

מוזגים כוס שלישי ומברכים ברכת המזון.
Pour the third cup and recite the Grace after Meals.

שִׁיר הַמַּעֲלוֹת, בְּשׁוּב ה' אֶת שִׁיבַת צִיּוֹן הָיִינוּ כְּחֹלְמִים. אָז יִמָּלֵא שְׂחוֹק פִּינוּ וּלְשׁוֹנֵנוּ רִנָּה. אָז יֹאמְרוּ בַגּוֹיִם: הִגְדִּיל ה' לַעֲשׂוֹת עִם אֵלֶּה. הִגְדִּיל ה' לַעֲשׂוֹת עִמָּנוּ, הָיִינוּ שְׂמֵחִים. שׁוּבָה ה' אֶת שְׁבִיתֵנוּ כַּאֲפִיקִים בַּנֶּגֶב. הַזֹּרְעִים בְּדִמְעָה, בְּרִנָּה יִקְצֹרוּ. הָלוֹךְ יֵלֵךְ וּבָכֹה נֹשֵׂא מֶשֶׁךְ הַזָּרַע, בֹּא יָבֹא בְרִנָּה נֹשֵׂא אֲלֻמֹּתָיו.

A Song of Ascents: When the Lord brings back the captivity of Zion, we will be like dreamers. Then our mouth will be full of mirth and our tongue joyful melody; then they will say among the nations, "The Lord has done greatly with these people." The Lord has done great things with us; we are happy. Lord, return us from captivity like streams in the desert. Those that sow with tears will reap with joyful song. The one who goes and cries carries the measure of seed; that person will surely come in joyful song bearing sheaves. (Psalms 126)

שלושה שאכלו כאחד חייבים לזמן והמזמן פותח (וכשהם עשרה יש להוסיף את הכתוב בסוגריים):
If three or more people are present, begin here (if ten or more are present, insert the bracketed additions):

רַבּוֹתַי נְבָרֵךְ:

My associates, let us bless:

המסובים עונים:
All those present answer:

יְהִי שֵׁם ה' מְבֹרָךְ מֵעַתָּה וְעַד עוֹלָם.

May the name of the Lord be blessed from now and forever. (Psalms 113:2)

המזמן אומר:
The leader says:

בִּרְשׁוּת מָרָנָן וְרַבָּנָן וְרַבּוֹתַי, נְבָרֵךְ [אֱלֹהֵינוּ] שֶׁאָכַלְנוּ מִשֶּׁלּוֹ.

WITH the permission of our companions and our teachers and my associates, let us bless [our God] from whom we have eaten.

המסבים עונים:
Those present answer:

בָּרוּךְ [אֱלֹהֵינוּ] שֶׁאָכַלְנוּ מִשֶּׁלּוֹ וּבְטוּבוֹ חָיִינוּ

BLESSED is [our God] from whom we have eaten and from whose goodness we live.

המזמן חוזר ואומר:
The leader repeats and says:

בָּרוּךְ [אֱלֹהֵינוּ] שֶׁאָכַלְנוּ מִשֶּׁלּוֹ וּבְטוּבוֹ חָיִינוּ

BLESSED is [our God] from whom we have eaten and from whose goodness we live.

כלם אומרים:
All say:

בָּרוּךְ אַתָּה ה׳, אֱלֹהֵינוּ מֶלֶךְ הָעוֹלָם, הַזָּן אֶת הָעוֹלָם כֻּלּוֹ בְּטוּבוֹ בְּחֵן בְּחֶסֶד וּבְרַחֲמִים, הוּא נוֹתֵן לֶחֶם לְכָל בָּשָׂר כִּי לְעוֹלָם חַסְדּוֹ. וּבְטוּבוֹ הַגָּדוֹל תָּמִיד לֹא חָסַר לָנוּ, וְאַל יֶחְסַר לָנוּ מָזוֹן לְעוֹלָם וָעֶד. בַּעֲבוּר שְׁמוֹ הַגָּדוֹל, כִּי הוּא אֵל זָן וּמְפַרְנֵס לַכֹּל וּמֵטִיב לַכֹּל, וּמֵכִין מָזוֹן לְכָל בְּרִיּוֹתָיו אֲשֶׁר בָּרָא. בָּרוּךְ אַתָּה ה׳, הַזָּן אֶת הַכֹּל.

BLESSED are You, Lord our God, Sovereign of the universe, who nourishes the entire world in His goodness, in grace, in kindness, and in mercy. He gives bread to all flesh, since His kindness endures forever. And in His great goodness, we have never lacked. And may we not lack nourishment forever and always, because of His great name, since He is God that feeds and provides for all and does good to all and prepares nourishment for all the creatures that he created. Blessed are You, Lord, who sustains all.

נוֹדֶה לְךָ ה׳ אֱלֹהֵינוּ עַל שֶׁהִנְחַלְתָּ לַאֲבוֹתֵינוּ אֶרֶץ חֶמְדָּה טוֹבָה וּרְחָבָה, וְעַל שֶׁהוֹצֵאתָנוּ ה׳ אֱלֹהֵינוּ מֵאֶרֶץ מִצְרַיִם, וּפְדִיתָנוּ מִבֵּית עֲבָדִים, וְעַל בְּרִיתְךָ שֶׁחָתַמְתָּ בִּבְשָׂרֵנוּ, וְעַל תּוֹרָתְךָ שֶׁלִּמַּדְתָּנוּ, וְעַל חֻקֶּיךָ שֶׁהוֹדַעְתָּנוּ, וְעַל חַיִּים חֵן וָחֶסֶד שֶׁחוֹנַנְתָּנוּ, וְעַל אֲכִילַת מָזוֹן שֶׁאַתָּה זָן וּמְפַרְנֵס אוֹתָנוּ תָּמִיד, בְּכָל יוֹם וּבְכָל עֵת וּבְכָל שָׁעָה:

וְעַל הַכֹּל ה׳ אֱלֹהֵינוּ, אֲנַחְנוּ מוֹדִים לָךְ וּמְבָרְכִים אוֹתָךְ, יִתְבָּרַךְ שִׁמְךָ בְּפִי כָּל חַי תָּמִיד לְעוֹלָם וָעֶד. כַּכָּתוּב: וְאָכַלְתָּ וְשָׂבַעְתָּ וּבֵרַכְתָּ אֶת ה׳ אֱלֹהֶיךָ עַל הָאָרֶץ הַטּוֹבָה אֲשֶׁר נָתַן לָךְ. בָּרוּךְ אַתָּה ה׳, עַל הָאָרֶץ וְעַל הַמָּזוֹן.

רַחֵם נָא ה׳ אֱלֹהֵינוּ עַל יִשְׂרָאֵל עַמֶּךָ וְעַל יְרוּשָׁלַיִם עִירֶךָ וְעַל צִיּוֹן מִשְׁכַּן כְּבוֹדֶךָ וְעַל מַלְכוּת בֵּית דָּוִד מְשִׁיחֶךָ וְעַל הַבַּיִת הַגָּדוֹל וְהַקָּדוֹשׁ שֶׁנִּקְרָא שִׁמְךָ עָלָיו: אֱלֹהֵינוּ אָבִינוּ, רְעֵנוּ זוּנֵנוּ פַּרְנְסֵנוּ וְכַלְכְּלֵנוּ וְהַרְוִיחֵנוּ, וְהַרְוַח לָנוּ ה׳ אֱלֹהֵינוּ מְהֵרָה מִכָּל צָרוֹתֵינוּ. וְנָא אַל תַּצְרִיכֵנוּ ה׳ אֱלֹהֵינוּ, לֹא לִידֵי מַתְּנַת בָּשָׂר וָדָם וְלֹא לִידֵי הַלְוָאָתָם, כִּי אִם לְיָדְךָ הַמְּלֵאָה הַפְּתוּחָה הַקְּדוֹשָׁה וְהָרְחָבָה, שֶׁלֹּא נֵבוֹשׁ וְלֹא נִכָּלֵם לְעוֹלָם וָעֶד.

WE thank You, Lord our God, for having given as an inheritance to our ancestors a lovely, good, and broad land, and for having taken us out, Lord our God, from the land of Egypt, and for redeeming us from the house of slavery, and for Your covenant that You have sealed in our flesh, and for Your Torah that You have taught us, and for Your statutes that You have made known to us, and for the life, grace, and kindness that You have granted us, and for the nourishment that You feed us and provide for us always, on all days, at all times, and in every hour.

AND for everything, Lord our God, we thank You and bless You. May Your name be blessed by the mouth of all life, constantly, forever and always, as it is written, "You shall eat and you shall be satiated and you shall bless the Lord your God for the good land that He has given you" (Deuteronomy 8:10). Blessed are You, Lord, for the land and for the nourishment.

PLEASE have mercy, Lord our God, upon Israel, Your people, and upon Jerusalem, Your city, and upon Zion, the dwelling place of Your Glory, and upon the monarchy of the House of David, Your appointed one, and upon the great and holy house that is called by Your name. Our God, our Father, tend to us, sustain us, provide for us, relieve us, and give us quick reprieve, Lord our God, from all of our troubles. And please do not make us dependent, Lord our God, on the gifts of flesh and blood nor on their loans – but instead on Your full, open, holy, and abundant hand, so that we are not humiliated or ashamed, forever and always.

בשבת מוסיפים:
On Shabbat, add the following paragraph:

רְצֵה וְהַחֲלִיצֵנוּ ה׳ אֱלֹהֵינוּ בְּמִצְוֹתֶיךָ וּבְמִצְוַת יוֹם הַשְּׁבִיעִי הַשַּׁבָּת הַגָּדוֹל וְהַקָּדוֹשׁ הַזֶּה. כִּי יוֹם זֶה גָּדוֹל וְקָדוֹשׁ הוּא לְפָנֶיךָ לִשְׁבָּת בּוֹ וְלָנוּחַ בּוֹ בְּאַהֲבָה כְּמִצְוַת רְצוֹנֶךָ. וּבִרְצוֹנְךָ הָנִיחַ לָנוּ ה׳ אֱלֹהֵינוּ שֶׁלֹּא תְהֵא צָרָה וְיָגוֹן וַאֲנָחָה בְּיוֹם מְנוּחָתֵנוּ. וְהַרְאֵנוּ ה׳ אֱלֹהֵינוּ בְּנֶחָמַת צִיּוֹן עִירֶךָ וּבְבִנְיַן יְרוּשָׁלַיִם עִיר קָדְשֶׁךָ כִּי אַתָּה הוּא בַּעַל הַיְשׁוּעוֹת וּבַעַל הַנֶּחָמוֹת.

MAY it please You to strengthen us, Lord our God, in Your commandments and in the commandment of the seventh day, this great and holy Shabbat. For this day is great and holy before You, to cease work on it and to rest on it, with love, according to the commandment of Your will. And with Your will, allow us, Lord our God, to have no trouble, grief, or sorrow on the day of our rest. And may You show us, Lord our God, the consolation of Zion, Your city, and the building of Jerusalem, Your holy city. For You are the Master of salvations and the Master of consolations.

אֱלֹהֵינוּ וֵאלֹהֵי אֲבוֹתֵינוּ, יַעֲלֶה וְיָבֹא וְיַגִּיעַ וְיֵרָאֶה וְיֵרָצֶה וְיִשָּׁמַע וְיִפָּקֵד וְיִזָּכֵר זִכְרוֹנֵנוּ וּפִקְדוֹנֵנוּ, וְזִכְרוֹן אֲבוֹתֵינוּ, וְזִכְרוֹן מָשִׁיחַ בֶּן דָּוִד עַבְדֶּךָ, וְזִכְרוֹן יְרוּשָׁלַיִם עִיר קָדְשֶׁךָ, וְזִכְרוֹן כָּל עַמְּךָ בֵּית יִשְׂרָאֵל לְפָנֶיךָ, לִפְלֵיטָה לְטוֹבָה לְחֵן וּלְחֶסֶד וּלְרַחֲמִים, לְחַיִּים וּלְשָׁלוֹם בְּיוֹם חַג הַמַּצּוֹת הַזֶּה זָכְרֵנוּ ה׳ אֱלֹהֵינוּ בּוֹ לְטוֹבָה וּפָקְדֵנוּ בּוֹ לִבְרָכָה וְהוֹשִׁיעֵנוּ בּוֹ לְחַיִּים. וּבִדְבַר יְשׁוּעָה וְרַחֲמִים חוּס וְחָנֵּנוּ וְרַחֵם עָלֵינוּ וְהוֹשִׁיעֵנוּ, כִּי אֵלֶיךָ עֵינֵינוּ, כִּי אֵל מֶלֶךְ חַנּוּן וְרַחוּם אָתָּה.

GOD and God of our ancestors, may it ascend and come and reach and be seen and be acceptable and be heard and be recalled and be remembered – our remembrance and our recollection, and the remembrance of our ancestors, and the remembrance of the messiah, the son of David, Your servant, and the remembrance of Jerusalem, Your holy city, and the remembrance of all Your people, the House of Israel – in front of You, for survival, for good, for grace, for kindness, and for mercy, for life and for peace on this day of the Festival of Matzot. Remember us, Lord our God, on it for good, and recall us on it for survival, and save us on it for life – and by the word of salvation and mercy, pity and grace us, and have mercy on us and save us, since our eyes are upon You, as You are a graceful and merciful Ruler.

Jewish Quarter,
Jerusalem,
Israel, 1995

וּבְנֵה יְרוּשָׁלַיִם עִיר הַקֹּדֶשׁ בִּמְהֵרָה בְיָמֵינוּ. בָּרוּךְ אַתָּה ה', בּוֹנֵה בְרַחֲמָיו יְרוּשָׁלַיִם. אָמֵן.

AND may You build Jerusalem, the holy city, quickly and in our days. Blessed are You, Lord, who builds Jerusalem in His mercy. Amen.

בָּרוּךְ אַתָּה ה', אֱלֹהֵינוּ מֶלֶךְ הָעוֹלָם, הָאֵל אָבִינוּ מַלְכֵּנוּ אַדִירֵנוּ בּוֹרְאֵנוּ גּוֹאֲלֵנוּ יוֹצְרֵנוּ קְדוֹשֵׁנוּ קְדוֹשׁ יַעֲקֹב רוֹעֵנוּ רוֹעֵה יִשְׂרָאֵל הַמֶּלֶךְ הַטּוֹב וְהַמֵּטִיב לַכֹּל שֶׁבְּכָל יוֹם וָיוֹם הוּא הֵטִיב, הוּא מֵטִיב, הוּא יֵיטִיב לָנוּ. הוּא גְמָלָנוּ הוּא גוֹמְלֵנוּ הוּא יִגְמְלֵנוּ לָעַד, לְחֵן וּלְחֶסֶד וּלְרַחֲמִים וּלְרֶוַח הַצָּלָה וְהַצְלָחָה, בְּרָכָה וִישׁוּעָה נֶחָמָה פַּרְנָסָה וְכַלְכָּלָה וְרַחֲמִים וְחַיִּים וְשָׁלוֹם וְכָל טוֹב, וּמִכָּל טוּב לְעוֹלָם אַל יְחַסְּרֵנוּ.

BLESSED are You, Lord our God, Sovereign of the universe, God, our Father, our Sovereign, our Mighty One, our Creator, our Redeemer, our Shaper, our Holy One, the Holy One of Ya'akov, our shepherd, the shepherd of Israel, the good Sovereign, who does good to all. On every single day He has done good, He does good, He will do good to us. He has granted us, He grants us, He will grant us forever – in grace and in kindness and in mercy and in relief – rescue and success, blessing and salvation, consolation, provision and relief and mercy and life and peace and all good; and may we not lack any good ever.

הָרַחֲמָן הוּא יִמְלֹךְ עָלֵינוּ לְעוֹלָם וָעֶד. הָרַחֲמָן הוּא יִתְבָּרַךְ בַּשָּׁמַיִם וּבָאָרֶץ. הָרַחֲמָן הוּא יִשְׁתַּבַּח לְדוֹר דּוֹרִים, וְיִתְפָּאַר בָּנוּ לָעַד וּלְנֵצַח נְצָחִים, וְיִתְהַדַּר בָּנוּ לָעַד וּלְעוֹלְמֵי עוֹלָמִים. הָרַחֲמָן הוּא יְפַרְנְסֵנוּ בְּכָבוֹד. הָרַחֲמָן הוּא יִשְׁבּוֹר עֻלֵּנוּ מֵעַל צַוָּארֵנוּ, וְהוּא יוֹלִיכֵנוּ קוֹמְמִיּוּת לְאַרְצֵנוּ. הָרַחֲמָן הוּא יִשְׁלַח לָנוּ בְּרָכָה מְרֻבָּה בַּבַּיִת הַזֶּה, וְעַל שֻׁלְחָן זֶה שֶׁאָכַלְנוּ עָלָיו. הָרַחֲמָן הוּא יִשְׁלַח לָנוּ אֶת אֵלִיָּהוּ הַנָּבִיא זָכוּר לַטּוֹב, וִיבַשֶּׂר לָנוּ בְּשׂוֹרוֹת טוֹבוֹת יְשׁוּעוֹת וְנֶחָמוֹת.

MAY the Merciful One reign over us forever and always. May the Merciful One be blessed in the heavens and in the earth. May the Merciful One be praised for all generations, and exalted among us forever and ever, and glorified among us always and infinitely for all infinities. May the Merciful One sustain us honorably. May the Merciful One break our yolk from upon our necks and bring us upright to our land. May the Merciful One send us multiple blessings, to this home and on this table upon which we have eaten. May the Merciful One send us Eliyahu the prophet – may he be remembered for good – who shall announce to us tidings of good, of salvation, and of consolation.

הָרַחֲמָן הוּא יְבָרֵךְ אוֹתִי [וְאֶת בַּעֲלִי / אִשְׁתִּי וְאֶת זַרְעִי] וְאֶת כָּל אֲשֶׁר לִי. הָרַחֲמָן הוּא יְבָרֵךְ אֶת [אָבִי מוֹרִי] בַּעַל הַבַּיִת הַזֶּה. וְאֶת [אִמִּי מוֹרָתִי] בַּעֲלַת הַבַּיִת הַזֶּה, אוֹתָם וְאֶת בֵּיתָם וְאֶת זַרְעָם וְאֶת כָּל אֲשֶׁר לָהֶם. אוֹתָנוּ וְאֶת כָּל אֲשֶׁר לָנוּ, כְּמוֹ שֶׁנִּתְבָּרְכוּ אֲבוֹתֵינוּ אַבְרָהָם יִצְחָק וְיַעֲקֹב בַּכֹּל מִכֹּל כֹּל, כֵּן יְבָרֵךְ אוֹתָנוּ כֻּלָּנוּ יַחַד בִּבְרָכָה שְׁלֵמָה, וְנֹאמַר אָמֵן.

MAY the Merciful One bless me [and my husband/my wife and my children] and all that is mine. May the Merciful One bless [my father, my teacher,] the master of this home and [my mother, my teacher,] the mistress of this home, they and their home and their offspring and everything that is theirs, us and all that is ours. As were blessed Avraham, Yitzchak, and Ya'akov, in everything, from everything, with everything, so too should He bless us, all of us together, with a complete blessing, and we shall say, Amen.

בַּמָּרוֹם יְלַמְּדוּ עֲלֵיהֶם וְעָלֵינוּ זְכוּת שֶׁתְּהֵא לְמִשְׁמֶרֶת שָׁלוֹם. וְנִשָּׂא בְרָכָה מֵאֵת ה', וּצְדָקָה מֵאֱלֹהֵי יִשְׁעֵנוּ, וְנִמְצָא חֵן וְשֵׂכֶל טוֹב בְּעֵינֵי אֱלֹהִים וְאָדָם. [בשבת: הָרַחֲמָן הוּא יַנְחִילֵנוּ יוֹם שֶׁכֻּלוֹ שַׁבָּת וּמְנוּחָה לְחַיֵּי הָעוֹלָמִים.] הָרַחֲמָן הוּא יַנְחִילֵנוּ יוֹם שֶׁכֻּלוֹ טוֹב [יוֹם שֶׁכֻּלוֹ אָרוּךְ. יוֹם שֶׁצַּדִּיקִים יוֹשְׁבִים וְעַטְרוֹתֵיהֶם בְּרָאשֵׁיהֶם וְנֶהֱנִים מִזִּיו הַשְּׁכִינָה וִיהִי חֶלְקֵנוּ עִמָּהֶם].

IN the heavens, may they invoke upon them and upon us merit that will protect us in peace. And may we carry a blessing from the Lord and charity from the God of our salvation, and find grace and good understanding in the eyes of God and man. [On Shabbat, we say: May the Merciful One grant us the inheritance of the day of complete Shabbat and rest in everlasting life.] May the Merciful One grant us the inheritance of the festival day.

הָרַחֲמָן הוּא יְזַכֵּנוּ לִימוֹת הַמָּשִׁיחַ וּלְחַיֵּי הָעוֹלָם הַבָּא. מִגְדּוֹל יְשׁוּעוֹת מַלְכּוֹ וְעֹשֶׂה חֶסֶד לִמְשִׁיחוֹ לְדָוִד וּלְזַרְעוֹ עַד עוֹלָם. עֹשֶׂה שָׁלוֹם בִּמְרוֹמָיו, הוּא יַעֲשֶׂה שָׁלוֹם עָלֵינוּ וְעַל כָּל יִשְׂרָאֵל וְאִמְרוּ אָמֵן.

MAY the Merciful One give us merit for the times of the messiah and for life in the world to come. A tower of salvations is our Sovereign; may He do kindness with His messiah, with David and his offspring, forever (II Samuel 22:51). The One who makes peace above, may He make peace upon us and upon all of Israel; and we say, Amen.

יְראוּ אֶת ה׳ קְדשָׁיו, כִּי אֵין מַחְסוֹר לִירֵאָיו. כְּפִירִים רָשׁוּ וְרָעֵבוּ, וְדֹרְשֵׁי ה׳ לֹא יַחְסְרוּ כָל טוֹב. הוֹדוּ לַה׳ כִּי טוֹב כִּי לְעוֹלָם חַסְדּוֹ. פּוֹתֵחַ אֶת יָדֶךָ, וּמַשְׂבִּיעַ לְכָל חַי רָצוֹן. בָּרוּךְ הַגֶּבֶר אֲשֶׁר יִבְטַח בַּה׳, וְהָיָה ה׳ מִבְטַחוֹ. נַעַר הָיִיתִי גַּם זָקַנְתִּי, וְלֹא רָאִיתִי צַדִּיק נֶעֱזָב, וְזַרְעוֹ מְבַקֶּשׁ לָחֶם. ה׳ עֹז לְעַמּוֹ יִתֵּן, ה׳ יְבָרֵךְ אֶת עַמּוֹ בַשָּׁלוֹם.

FEAR the Lord, His holy ones, since there is no lacking for those that fear Him. Young lions may go without and suffer hunger, but those who seek the Lord will not lack any good thing. (Psalms 34:10–11) Thank the Lord, since He is good, since His kindness endures forever. (Psalms 118:1) You open Your hand and satisfy the will of all living things. (Psalms 145:16) Blessed is the man who trusts in the Lord and makes the Lord his security. (Jeremiah 17:7) I was a youth and I have become old and I have not seen a righteous person forsaken or his offspring begging for bread. (Psalms 37:25) The Lord will give courage to His people. The Lord will bless His people with peace. (Psalms 29:11)

כוס שלישית
Kos Shlishit: Third Cup of Wine

בָּרוּךְ אַתָּה ה', אֱלֹהֵינוּ מֶלֶךְ הָעוֹלָם בּוֹרֵא פְּרִי הַגָּפֶן.

BLESSED *are You, Lord our God, Sovereign of the universe, who creates the fruit of the vine.*

Wine Cellar, Samarkand, Uzbekistan, 1998

ושותה בהסבה ואינו מברך ברכה אחרונה.
Drink while reclining, and do not say a blessing afterwards.

שפוך חמתך
Shfoch Chamatcha: Pour Out Your Wrath

מוזגים כוס של אליהו ופותחים את הדלת:
Fill the cup of Eliyahu and open the door.

שְׁפֹךְ חֲמָתְךָ אֶל־הַגּוֹיִם אֲשֶׁר לֹא יְדָעוּךָ וְעַל־מַמְלָכוֹת אֲשֶׁר בְּשִׁמְךָ לֹא קָרָאוּ. כִּי אָכַל אֶת־יַעֲקֹב וְאֶת־נָוֵהוּ הֵשַׁמּוּ. שְׁפָךְ־עֲלֵיהֶם זַעְמֶךָ וַחֲרוֹן אַפְּךָ יַשִּׂיגֵם. תִּרְדֹּף בְּאַף וְתַשְׁמִידֵם מִתַּחַת שְׁמֵי ה'.

POUR out your wrath on the nations that have not known You and upon the kingdoms that have not called on Your name! For they have consumed Ya'akov and laid waste to his habitation. (Psalms 79:6–7) Pour out Your fury upon them, and the fierceness of Your anger shall reach them! (Psalms 69:25) Pursue them with anger and eradicate them from under the skies of the Lord. (Lamentations 3:66)

Pour Out Your Wrath

The Seder encapsulates almost all of what Jews – from the most learned to the completely untutored – love about their tradition: ritual, good food, family, and friends. There is one paragraph, a relatively short one, that has, in recent years, left many Jews discomforted. It comes, traditionally, after the meal, when those gathered around the table implore God to "Pour out your wrath on the nations that have not known You and upon the kingdoms that have not called on Your name! For they have consumed Ya'akov and laid waste to his habitation."

For many contemporary Jews, this is a paragraph worth skipping. Some have altered it to read, "Pour out Your love on the nations that do not know You." They find the original bloodthirsty and violent. It is not who they see themselves to be.

In contrast to these folks, I may well rank this as one of my favorite paragraphs in the Haggadah. First of all, it is full of qualifiers. It does not say, "Pour out Your wrath on all the nations that do not know You," i.e., all non-Jews. It asks for punishment for those who have tried to destroy Your people. This is not an attack on nonbelievers. It is an attack on those who would murder, pillage, and destroy. Moreover, it does not say: "God give me strength to pour out my wrath. Give me the opportunity to exact revenge." It is not a matter of personal revenge.

Today this paragraph is read when we open the door for Elijah. Given that Elijah, tradition has it, appears at every

91

Seder, it seems strange that he would need the door opened. In fact, there are those who say the door used to be opened at the very beginning of the Seder, at the time we recited "*ha lachma anya*," the invitation to all who are hungry to come and join us to eat. If you are going to invite someone in, you do it with the door open.

The problem was that, given the Christian antisemitic myth that this was the night Jews celebrated by using the blood of children in their matzah, this was a dangerous night for Jews. Therefore, to open the door at that moment, when more people were out and about, was not prudent. Hence, the door opening was moved to later in the Seder when it is safer to open it, because those who might harm us had gone home for the night.

If this is correct, then there is a certain irony here. We stand and boldly ask God to punish those who have persecuted us. Even though our voices are full of strength, vigor, and demands for justice, we have prudently refrained from opening the door when we were more vulnerable. Calls for righteous justice and a reminder of our historic extreme vulnerability come together at this moment in the Seder.

– Prof. Deborah E. Lipstadt, PhD

Elijah's Chair,
Kokand,
Uzbekistan, 1999

הַלֵּל
HALLEL: SAY HALLEL

מוזגים כוס רביעית וגומרים את ההלל.
Pour the fourth cup and complete the Hallel.

לֹא לָנוּ, ה׳, לֹא לָנוּ, כִּי לְשִׁמְךָ תֵּן כָּבוֹד, עַל חַסְדְּךָ עַל אֲמִתֶּךָ. לָמָּה יֹאמְרוּ הַגּוֹיִם אַיֵּה נָא אֱלֹהֵיהֶם. וֵאלֹהֵינוּ בַשָּׁמַיִם, כֹּל אֲשֶׁר חָפֵץ עָשָׂה. עֲצַבֵּיהֶם כֶּסֶף וְזָהָב מַעֲשֵׂה יְדֵי אָדָם. פֶּה לָהֶם וְלֹא יְדַבֵּרוּ, עֵינַיִם לָהֶם וְלֹא יִרְאוּ. אָזְנַיִם לָהֶם וְלֹא יִשְׁמָעוּ, אַף לָהֶם וְלֹא יְרִיחוּן. יְדֵיהֶם וְלֹא יְמִישׁוּן, רַגְלֵיהֶם וְלֹא יְהַלֵּכוּ, לֹא יֶהְגּוּ בִּגְרוֹנָם. כְּמוֹהֶם יִהְיוּ עֹשֵׂיהֶם, כֹּל אֲשֶׁר בֹּטֵחַ בָּהֶם. יִשְׂרָאֵל בְּטַח בַּיי, עֶזְרָם וּמָגִנָּם הוּא. בֵּית אַהֲרֹן בִּטְחוּ בַיי, עֶזְרָם וּמָגִנָּם הוּא. יִרְאֵי ה׳ בִּטְחוּ בַיי, עֶזְרָם וּמָגִנָּם הוּא. ה׳ זְכָרָנוּ יְבָרֵךְ. יְבָרֵךְ אֶת בֵּית יִשְׂרָאֵל, יְבָרֵךְ אֶת בֵּית אַהֲרֹן, יְבָרֵךְ יִרְאֵי ה׳, הַקְּטַנִּים עִם הַגְּדֹלִים. יֹסֵף ה׳ עֲלֵיכֶם, עֲלֵיכֶם וְעַל בְּנֵיכֶם. בְּרוּכִים אַתֶּם לַיי, עֹשֵׂה שָׁמַיִם וָאָרֶץ. הַשָּׁמַיִם שָׁמַיִם לַה׳ וְהָאָרֶץ נָתַן לִבְנֵי אָדָם. לֹא הַמֵּתִים יְהַלְלוּ יָהּ וְלֹא כָּל יֹרְדֵי דוּמָה. וַאֲנַחְנוּ נְבָרֵךְ יָהּ מֵעַתָּה וְעַד עוֹלָם. הַלְלוּיָהּ.

אָהַבְתִּי כִּי יִשְׁמַע ה׳ אֶת קוֹלִי תַּחֲנוּנָי. כִּי הִטָּה אָזְנוֹ לִי וּבְיָמַי אֶקְרָא. אֲפָפוּנִי חֶבְלֵי מָוֶת וּמְצָרֵי שְׁאוֹל מְצָאוּנִי, צָרָה וְיָגוֹן אֶמְצָא. וּבְשֵׁם ה׳ אֶקְרָא: אָנָּא ה׳ מַלְּטָה נַפְשִׁי. חַנּוּן ה׳ וְצַדִּיק, וֵאלֹהֵינוּ מְרַחֵם. שֹׁמֵר פְּתָאיִם ה׳, דַּלּוֹתִי וְלִי יְהוֹשִׁיעַ. שׁוּבִי נַפְשִׁי לִמְנוּחָיְכִי, כִּי ה׳ גָּמַל עָלָיְכִי. כִּי חִלַּצְתָּ נַפְשִׁי מִמָּוֶת, אֶת עֵינִי מִן דִּמְעָה, אֶת רַגְלִי מִדֶּחִי. אֶתְהַלֵּךְ לִפְנֵי ה׳ בְּאַרְצוֹת הַחַיִּים. הֶאֱמַנְתִּי כִּי אֲדַבֵּר, אֲנִי עָנִיתִי מְאֹד. אֲנִי אָמַרְתִּי בְחָפְזִי כָּל הָאָדָם כֹּזֵב.

מָה אָשִׁיב לַה׳ כֹּל תַּגְמוּלוֹהִי עָלָי. כּוֹס יְשׁוּעוֹת אֶשָּׂא וּבְשֵׁם ה׳ אֶקְרָא. נְדָרַי לַה׳ אֲשַׁלֵּם נֶגְדָה נָּא לְכָל עַמּוֹ. יָקָר בְּעֵינֵי ה׳ הַמָּוְתָה לַחֲסִידָיו. אָנָּה ה׳ כִּי אֲנִי עַבְדֶּךָ, אֲנִי עַבְדְּךָ בֶּן אֲמָתֶךָ, פִּתַּחְתָּ לְמוֹסֵרָי. לְךָ אֶזְבַּח זֶבַח תּוֹדָה וּבְשֵׁם ה׳ אֶקְרָא. נְדָרַי לַה׳ אֲשַׁלֵּם נֶגְדָה נָּא לְכָל עַמּוֹ. בְּחַצְרוֹת בֵּית ה׳, בְּתוֹכֵכִי יְרוּשָׁלַיִם. הַלְלוּיָהּ.

NOT *to us, not to us, but rather to Your name, give glory, for Your kindness and for Your truth. Why should the nations say, "Say, where is their God?" Our God is in the heavens; all that He wanted He has done. Their idols are silver and gold, the work of men's hands. They have a mouth but do not speak; they have eyes but do not see. They have ears but do not hear; they have a nose but do not smell; hands, but do not feel; feet, but* *do not walk; they do not make a peep from their throat. Like them will be their makers, all those that trust in them. Israel must trust in the Lord; their help and shield is He. The House of Aharon must trust in the Lord; their help and shield is He. Those that fear the Lord must trust in the Lord; their help and shield is He. The Lord who remembers us will bless; He will bless the House of Israel; He will bless the House of Aharon. He will bless those who fear the Lord, the small ones with the great ones. May the Lord add to your bounty – yours and your children's. Blessed are you to the Lord, the Maker of the heavens and the earth. The heavens are the Lord's heavens, but the earth He has given to the children of humanity. It is not the dead who will praise the Lord, and not those who go down in silence. But we will bless the Lord from now and forever. Halleluyah! (Psalms 115)*

I love that the Lord hears my voice, my supplications. Because He has inclined His ear to me, I will call out to Him all my days. The bonds of death encircled me, and the confines of the grave seized me; agony and grief I found. But in the name of the Lord I called out, "Please Lord, spare my soul." Gracious is the Lord and righteous; and our God acts mercifully. The Lord watches over the simple; I was low and He has saved me. Return, O my soul, to rest, because the Lord has favored you. For You have rescued my soul from death, my eyes from tears, my feet from stumbling. I will walk before the Lord in the lands of the living. I have trusted, even as I said, "I am very afflicted." I spoke in haste; all men are deceitful. (Psalms 116:1–11)

WHAT can I give back to the Lord for all that He has favored me? A cup of salvations I will raise up, and I will call out in the name of the Lord. My vows to the Lord I will pay, now in front of His entire people. Precious in the eyes of the Lord is the death of His pious ones. O Lord, I am Your servant, the son of Your maidservant; You have opened my chains. To You will I offer a thanksgiving sacrifice, and I will call out in the name of the Lord. My vows to the Lord I will fulfill, now in front of His entire people, in the courtyards of the House of the Lord, in the midst of Jerusalem. Halleluyah! (Psalms 116:12–19)

הַלְלוּ אֶת ה׳ כָּל גּוֹיִם, שַׁבְּחוּהוּ כָּל הָאֻמִּים. כִּי גָבַר עָלֵינוּ חַסְדּוֹ, וֶאֱמֶת ה׳ לְעוֹלָם. הַלְלוּיָהּ. הוֹדוּ לַה׳ כִּי טוֹב כִּי לְעוֹלָם חַסְדּוֹ. יֹאמַר נָא יִשְׂרָאֵל כִּי לְעוֹלָם חַסְדּוֹ. יֹאמְרוּ נָא בֵית אַהֲרֹן כִּי לְעוֹלָם חַסְדּוֹ. יֹאמְרוּ נָא יִרְאֵי ה׳ כִּי לְעוֹלָם חַסְדּוֹ.

PRAISE the name of the Lord, all nations; extol Him, all peoples. For His kindness has overwhelmed us, and the truth of the Lord is forever. Halleluyah! Thank the Lord, for He is good, for His kindness endures forever. Let Israel now say, "Thank the Lord, for He is good, for His kindness endures forever." Let the House of Aharon now say, "Thank the Lord, for He is good, for His kindness endures forever." Let those who fear the Lord now say, "Thank the Lord, for He is good, for His kindness endures forever." (Psalms 117:1–118:4)

מִן הַמֵּצַר קָרָאתִי יָּה, עָנָנִי בַמֶּרְחָב יָה. ה׳ לִי, לֹא אִירָא – מַה יַּעֲשֶׂה לִי אָדָם, ה׳ לִי בְּעֹזְרָי וַאֲנִי אֶרְאֶה בְשֹׂנְאָי. טוֹב לַחֲסוֹת בַּה׳ מִבְּטֹחַ בָּאָדָם. טוֹב לַחֲסוֹת בַּה׳ מִבְּטֹחַ בִּנְדִיבִים. כָּל גּוֹיִם סְבָבוּנִי, בְּשֵׁם ה׳ כִּי אֲמִילַם. סַבּוּנִי גַם סְבָבוּנִי, בְּשֵׁם ה׳ כִּי אֲמִילַם. סַבּוּנִי כִדְבֹרִים, דֹּעֲכוּ כְּאֵשׁ קוֹצִים, בְּשֵׁם ה׳ כִּי אֲמִילַם. דָּחֹה דְחִיתַנִי לִנְפֹּל, וַה׳ עֲזָרָנִי. עָזִּי וְזִמְרָת יָּה וַיְהִי לִי לִישׁוּעָה. קוֹל רִנָּה וִישׁוּעָה בְּאָהֳלֵי צַדִּיקִים: יְמִין ה׳ עֹשָׂה חָיִל, יְמִין ה׳ רוֹמֵמָה, יְמִין ה׳ עֹשָׂה חָיִל. לֹא אָמוּת כִּי אֶחְיֶה, וַאֲסַפֵּר מַעֲשֵׂי יָהּ. יַסֹּר יִסְּרַנִּי יָּהּ, וְלַמָּוֶת לֹא נְתָנָנִי. פִּתְחוּ לִי שַׁעֲרֵי צֶדֶק, אָבֹא בָם, אוֹדֶה יָהּ. זֶה הַשַּׁעַר לַה׳, צַדִּיקִים יָבֹאוּ בוֹ.

אוֹדְךָ כִּי עֲנִיתָנִי וַתְּהִי לִי לִישׁוּעָה. אוֹדְךָ כִּי עֲנִיתָנִי וַתְּהִי לִי לִישׁוּעָה. אֶבֶן מָאֲסוּ הַבּוֹנִים הָיְתָה לְרֹאשׁ פִּנָּה. אֶבֶן מָאֲסוּ הַבּוֹנִים הָיְתָה לְרֹאשׁ פִּנָּה. מֵאֵת ה׳ הָיְתָה זֹּאת הִיא נִפְלָאת בְּעֵינֵינוּ. מֵאֵת ה׳ הָיְתָה זֹּאת הִיא נִפְלָאת בְּעֵינֵינוּ. זֶה הַיּוֹם עָשָׂה ה׳, נָגִילָה וְנִשְׂמְחָה בוֹ. זֶה הַיּוֹם עָשָׂה ה׳, נָגִילָה וְנִשְׂמְחָה בוֹ.

FROM *the straits, I have called the Lord; He answered me expansively. The Lord is with me; I will not fear – what can man do to me? The Lord is with me, with those who help me; and I will face those who hate me. It is better to take refuge with the Lord than to trust in man. It is better to take refuge with the Lord than to trust in nobles. All the nations surround me – in the name of the Lord, I will cut them down. They surround me, they encircled me – in the name of the Lord, I will cut them down. They surrounded me like bees, they were extinguished like a fire of thorns – in the name of the Lord, I will cut them down. They have surely pushed me to fall, but the Lord helped me. My strength and song is the Lord, and He has become my salvation. The sound of happy song and salvation is in the tents of the righteous; the right hand of the Lord acts powerfully. I will not die, but rather will live and recount the acts of the Lord. The Lord has surely chastised me, but He has not given me over to death. Open for me the gates of righteousness; I will enter them, thank the Lord. This is the gate of the Lord, the righteous will enter it. (Psalms 118:5–20)*

I *will give thanks to You, because You answered me and have become my salvation. The stone that was left by the builders has become the cornerstone. This was the work of the Lord; it is wondrous in our eyes. This is the day of the Lord; let us exult and rejoice on it. (Psalms 118:21–24)*

אָנָּא ה׳, הוֹשִׁיעָה נָּא. אָנָּא ה׳, הוֹשִׁיעָה נָּא. אָנָּא ה׳, הַצְלִיחָה נָּא. אָנָּא ה׳, הַצְלִיחָה נָּא.

Please, Lord, save us; please, Lord, enable us to succeed. (Psalms 118:25)

בָּרוּךְ הַבָּא בְּשֵׁם ה׳, בֵּרַכְנוּכֶם מִבֵּית ה׳. בָּרוּךְ הַבָּא בְּשֵׁם ה׳, בֵּרַכְנוּכֶם מִבֵּית ה׳. אֵל ה׳ וַיָּאֶר לָנוּ. אִסְרוּ חַג בַּעֲבֹתִים עַד קַרְנוֹת הַמִּזְבֵּחַ. אֵל ה׳ וַיָּאֶר לָנוּ. אִסְרוּ חַג בַּעֲבֹתִים עַד קַרְנוֹת הַמִּזְבֵּחַ. אֵלִי אַתָּה וְאוֹדֶךָּ, אֱלֹהַי – אֲרוֹמְמֶךָּ. אֵלִי אַתָּה וְאוֹדֶךָּ, אֱלֹהַי – אֲרוֹמְמֶךָּ. הוֹדוּ לַה׳ כִּי טוֹב, כִּי לְעוֹלָם חַסְדּוֹ. הוֹדוּ לַה׳ כִּי טוֹב, כִּי לְעוֹלָם חַסְדּוֹ.

יְהַלְלוּךָ ה׳ אֱלֹהֵינוּ כָּל מַעֲשֶׂיךָ, וַחֲסִידֶיךָ צַדִּיקִים עוֹשֵׂי רְצוֹנֶךָ, וְכָל עַמְּךָ בֵּית יִשְׂרָאֵל בְּרִנָּה יוֹדוּ וִיבָרְכוּ, וִישַׁבְּחוּ וִיפָאֲרוּ, וִירוֹמְמוּ וְיַעֲרִיצוּ, וְיַקְדִּישׁוּ וְיַמְלִיכוּ אֶת שִׁמְךָ, מַלְכֵּנוּ. כִּי לְךָ טוֹב לְהוֹדוֹת וּלְשִׁמְךָ נָאֶה לְזַמֵּר, כִּי מֵעוֹלָם וְעַד עוֹלָם אַתָּה אֵל.

BLESSED be the one who comes in the name of the Lord; we have blessed you from the House of the Lord. God is the Lord, and He has illuminated us; tie up the festival offering and bring it to the altar. You are my God, and I will thank You; my Lord, and I will exalt You. Thank the Lord, because He is good, because His kindness endures forever. (Psalms 118:26–29)

ALL of your works shall praise You, Lord our God, and your pious ones, the righteous ones who do Your will; and all of Your people, the House of Israel, will thank and bless in joyful song, and extol and glorify, and exalt and acclaim, and sanctify and coronate Your name, our Sovereign. For it is good to give thanks to You, and to Your name it is pleasant to sing, because you are God always and forever.

Debbie Friedman, Aspen, Colorado, USA, 1996

מזמורי הודיה
Mizmorei Hodayah: Songs of Praise and Thanks

הוֹדוּ לַה' כִּי טוֹב כִּי לְעוֹלָם חַסְדּוֹ. הוֹדוּ לֵאלֹהֵי הָאֱלֹהִים כִּי לְעוֹלָם חַסְדּוֹ. הוֹדוּ לַאֲדֹנֵי הָאֲדֹנִים כִּי לְעוֹלָם חַסְדּוֹ. לְעֹשֵׂה נִפְלָאוֹת גְּדֹלוֹת לְבַדּוֹ כִּי לְעוֹלָם חַסְדּוֹ. לְעֹשֵׂה הַשָּׁמַיִם בִּתְבוּנָה כִּי לְעוֹלָם חַסְדּוֹ. לְרוֹקַע הָאָרֶץ עַל הַמָּיִם כִּי לְעוֹלָם חַסְדּוֹ. לְעֹשֵׂה אוֹרִים גְּדֹלִים כִּי לְעוֹלָם חַסְדּוֹ. אֶת הַשֶּׁמֶשׁ לְמֶמְשֶׁלֶת בַּיּוֹם כִּי לְעוֹלָם חַסְדּוֹ. אֶת הַיָּרֵחַ וְכוֹכָבִים לְמֶמְשְׁלוֹת בַּלַּיְלָה כִּי לְעוֹלָם חַסְדּוֹ. לְמַכֵּה מִצְרַיִם בִּבְכוֹרֵיהֶם כִּי לְעוֹלָם חַסְדּוֹ. וַיּוֹצֵא יִשְׂרָאֵל מִתּוֹכָם כִּי לְעוֹלָם חַסְדּוֹ. בְּיָד חֲזָקָה וּבִזְרוֹעַ נְטוּיָה כִּי לְעוֹלָם חַסְדּוֹ. לְגֹזֵר יַם סוּף לִגְזָרִים כִּי לְעוֹלָם חַסְדּוֹ. וְהֶעֱבִיר יִשְׂרָאֵל בְּתוֹכוֹ כִּי לְעוֹלָם חַסְדּוֹ. וְנִעֵר פַּרְעֹה וְחֵילוֹ בְיַם סוּף כִּי לְעוֹלָם חַסְדּוֹ. לְמוֹלִיךְ עַמּוֹ בַּמִּדְבָּר כִּי לְעוֹלָם חַסְדּוֹ. לְמַכֵּה מְלָכִים גְּדֹלִים כִּי לְעוֹלָם חַסְדּוֹ. וַיַּהֲרֹג מְלָכִים אַדִּירִים כִּי לְעוֹלָם חַסְדּוֹ. לְסִיחוֹן מֶלֶךְ הָאֱמֹרִי כִּי לְעוֹלָם חַסְדּוֹ. וּלְעוֹג מֶלֶךְ הַבָּשָׁן כִּי לְעוֹלָם חַסְדּוֹ. וְנָתַן אַרְצָם לְנַחֲלָה כִּי לְעוֹלָם חַסְדּוֹ. נַחֲלָה לְיִשְׂרָאֵל עַבְדּוֹ כִּי לְעוֹלָם חַסְדּוֹ. שֶׁבְּשִׁפְלֵנוּ זָכַר לָנוּ כִּי לְעוֹלָם חַסְדּוֹ. וַיִּפְרְקֵנוּ מִצָּרֵינוּ כִּי לְעוֹלָם חַסְדּוֹ. נֹתֵן לֶחֶם לְכָל בָּשָׂר כִּי לְעוֹלָם חַסְדּוֹ. הוֹדוּ לְאֵל הַשָּׁמַיִם כִּי לְעוֹלָם חַסְדּוֹ.

THANK the Lord, for He is good, for His kindness endures forever. Thank the Lord of lords, for His kindness endures forever. To the Master of masters, for His kindness endures forever. To the One who alone does wondrously great deeds, for His kindness endures forever. To the one who made the Heavens with discernment, for His kindness endures forever. To the One who spread the earth over the waters, for His kindness endures forever. To the One who made the great lights, for His kindness endures forever; the sun to rule in the day, for His kindness endures forever; the moon and the stars to rule in the night, for His kindness endures forever. To the One who smote Egypt through their firstborn, for His kindness endures forever; and took Israel out from among them, for His kindness endures forever; with a strong hand and an outstretched arm, for His kindness endures forever. To the One who split the Red Sea, for His kindness endures forever; and led Israel through it, for His kindness endures forever; and drowned Pharaoh and his army in the Red Sea, for His kindness endures forever. To the One who led His people in the wilderness, for His kindness endures forever. To the One who smote great kings, for His kindness endures forever; and killed mighty kings, for His kindness endures forever; Sichon, king of the Amorites, for His kindness endures forever; and Og, king of Bashan, for His kindness endures forever; and gave their land as an inheritance, for His kindness endures forever; an inheritance for Israel His servant, for His kindness endures forever; that in our lowliness remembered us, for His kindness endures forever; and delivered us from our adversaries, for His kindness endures forever. He gives bread to all flesh, for His kindness endures forever. Thank the God of the heavens, for His kindness endures forever. (Psalms 136)

נִשְׁמַת כָּל חַי תְּבָרֵךְ אֶת שִׁמְךָ, ה' אֱלֹהֵינוּ, וְרוּחַ כָּל בָּשָׂר תְּפָאֵר וּתְרוֹמֵם זִכְרְךָ, מַלְכֵּנוּ, תָּמִיד. מִן הָעוֹלָם וְעַד הָעוֹלָם אַתָּה אֵל, וּמִבַּלְעָדֶיךָ אֵין לָנוּ מֶלֶךְ גּוֹאֵל וּמוֹשִׁיעַ, פּוֹדֶה וּמַצִּיל וּמְפַרְנֵס וּמְרַחֵם בְּכָל עֵת צָרָה וְצוּקָה. אֵין לָנוּ מֶלֶךְ אֶלָּא אַתָּה. אֱלֹהֵי הָרִאשׁוֹנִים וְהָאַחֲרוֹנִים, אֱלוֹהַּ כָּל בְּרִיּוֹת, אֲדוֹן כָּל תּוֹלָדוֹת, הַמְהֻלָּל בְּרֹב הַתִּשְׁבָּחוֹת, הַמְנַהֵג עוֹלָמוֹ בְּחֶסֶד וּבְרִיּוֹתָיו בְּרַחֲמִים. וַה' לֹא יָנוּם וְלֹא יִישָׁן – הַמְעוֹרֵר יְשֵׁנִים וְהַמֵּקִיץ נִרְדָּמִים, וְהַמֵּשִׂיחַ אִלְּמִים וְהַמַּתִּיר אֲסוּרִים וְהַסּוֹמֵךְ נוֹפְלִים וְהַזּוֹקֵף כְּפוּפִים. לְךָ לְבַדְּךָ אֲנַחְנוּ מוֹדִים.

אִלּוּ פִינוּ מָלֵא שִׁירָה כַיָּם, וּלְשׁוֹנֵנוּ רִנָּה כַּהֲמוֹן גַּלָּיו, וְשִׂפְתוֹתֵינוּ שֶׁבַח כְּמֶרְחֲבֵי רָקִיעַ, וְעֵינֵינוּ מְאִירוֹת כַּשֶּׁמֶשׁ וְכַיָּרֵחַ, וְיָדֵינוּ פְרוּשׂוֹת כְּנִשְׁרֵי שָׁמָיִם, וְרַגְלֵינוּ קַלּוֹת כָּאַיָּלוֹת – אֵין אֲנַחְנוּ מַסְפִּיקִים לְהוֹדוֹת לְךָ, ה' אֱלֹהֵינוּ וֵאלֹהֵי אֲבוֹתֵינוּ, וּלְבָרֵךְ אֶת שְׁמֶךָ עַל אַחַת מֵאֶלֶף, אַלְפֵי אֲלָפִים וְרִבֵּי רְבָבוֹת פְּעָמִים הַטּוֹבוֹת שֶׁעָשִׂיתָ עִם אֲבוֹתֵינוּ וְעִמָּנוּ. מִמִּצְרַיִם גְּאַלְתָּנוּ, ה' אֱלֹהֵינוּ, וּמִבֵּית עֲבָדִים פְּדִיתָנוּ, בְּרָעָב זַנְתָּנוּ וּבְשָׂבָע כִּלְכַּלְתָּנוּ, מֵחֶרֶב הִצַּלְתָּנוּ וּמִדֶּבֶר מִלַּטְתָּנוּ, וּמֵחֳלָיִם רָעִים וְנֶאֱמָנִים דִּלִּיתָנוּ.

עַד הֵנָּה עֲזָרוּנוּ רַחֲמֶיךָ וְלֹא עֲזָבוּנוּ חֲסָדֶיךָ, וְאַל תִּטְּשֵׁנוּ, ה' אֱלֹהֵינוּ, לָנֶצַח. עַל כֵּן אֵבָרִים שֶׁפִּלַּגְתָּ בָּנוּ וְרוּחַ וּנְשָׁמָה שֶׁנָּפַחְתָּ בְּאַפֵּינוּ וְלָשׁוֹן אֲשֶׁר שַׂמְתָּ בְּפִינוּ – הֵן הֵם יוֹדוּ וִיבָרְכוּ וִישַׁבְּחוּ וִיפָאֲרוּ וִירוֹמְמוּ וְיַעֲרִיצוּ וְיַקְדִּישׁוּ וְיַמְלִיכוּ אֶת שִׁמְךָ מַלְכֵּנוּ. כִּי כָל פֶּה לְךָ יוֹדֶה, וְכָל לָשׁוֹן לְךָ תִּשָּׁבַע, וְכָל בֶּרֶךְ לְךָ תִכְרַע, וְכָל קוֹמָה לְפָנֶיךָ תִשְׁתַּחֲוֶה, וְכָל לְבָבוֹת יִירָאוּךָ, וְכָל קֶרֶב וּכְלָיוֹת יְזַמְּרוּ לִשְׁמֶךָ. כַּדָּבָר שֶׁכָּתוּב, כָּל עַצְמֹתַי תֹּאמַרְנָה, ה' מִי כָמוֹךָ מַצִּיל עָנִי מֵחָזָק מִמֶּנּוּ וְעָנִי וְאֶבְיוֹן מִגֹּזְלוֹ. מִי יִדְמֶה לָּךְ וּמִי יִשְׁוֶה לָּךְ וּמִי יַעֲרָךְ לָךְ הָאֵל הַגָּדוֹל, הַגִּבּוֹר וְהַנּוֹרָא, אֵל עֶלְיוֹן, קֹנֵה שָׁמַיִם וָאָרֶץ. נְהַלֶּלְךָ וּנְשַׁבֵּחֲךָ וּנְפָאֶרְךָ וּנְבָרֵךְ אֶת שֵׁם קָדְשֶׁךָ, כָּאָמוּר: לְדָוִד, בָּרְכִי נַפְשִׁי אֶת ה' וְכָל קְרָבַי אֶת שֵׁם קָדְשׁוֹ. הָאֵל בְּתַעֲצֻמוֹת עֻזֶּךָ, הַגָּדוֹל בִּכְבוֹד שְׁמֶךָ, הַגִּבּוֹר לָנֶצַח וְהַנּוֹרָא בְּנוֹרְאוֹתֶיךָ, הַמֶּלֶךְ הַיּוֹשֵׁב עַל כִּסֵּא

רָם וְנִשָּׂא. שׁוֹכֵן עַד מָרוֹם וְקָדוֹשׁ שְׁמוֹ. וְכָתוּב: רַנְּנוּ צַדִּיקִים בַּיָי, לַיְשָׁרִים נָאוָה תְהִלָּה. בְּפִי יְשָׁרִים תִּתְהַלָּל, וּבְדִבְרֵי צַדִּיקִים תִּתְבָּרַךְ, וּבִלְשׁוֹן חֲסִידִים תִּתְרוֹמָם, וּבְקֶרֶב קְדוֹשִׁים תִּתְקַדָּשׁ.

THE soul of every living being shall bless Your name, Lord our God; the spirit of all flesh shall glorify and exalt Your fame always, our Sovereign. Forever and forever, You are God, and other than You we have no Sovereign, redeemer, or savior; You are a restorer, rescuer, provider, and merciful one in every moment of distress and anguish; we have no Sovereign besides You! God of the first ones and the last ones, God of all creatures, Master of all generations, who is praised through a multitude of praises, who guides His world with kindness and His creatures with mercy, the Lord who neither slumbers nor sleeps, He who rouses the sleepers and awakens the dozers, He who makes the mute speak, and frees the captives, and supports the fallen, and straightens the bent – we thank You alone.

WERE our mouth as full of song as the sea, and our tongue as full of joyous song as its multitude of waves, and our lips as full of praise as the breadth of the heavens, and our eyes as sparkling as the sun and the moon, and our hands as outspread as the eagles of the sky and our feet as swift as deer – we still could not thank You sufficiently, Lord our God and God of our ancestors, or bless Your name for a thousandth or a ten-thousandth of the goodness that You performed for our ancestors and for us. From Egypt, Lord our God, You redeemed us, and from the house of slavery You restored us. In famine You nourished us, and in plenty You sustained us. From the sword You saved us, and from plague You spared us; and from severe and enduring diseases You delivered us.

UNTIL now Your mercy has helped us, and Your kindness has not forsaken us; do not abandon us, Lord our God, ever. Therefore, the limbs that You set within us and the spirit and soul that You breathed into our nostrils, and the tongue that You placed in our mouth – indeed, they shall thank and bless and praise and glorify, and exalt and revere, and sanctify and coronate Your name, our Sovereign. For every mouth shall offer thanks to You, and every tongue shall swear allegiance to You, and every knee shall bend to You, and every upright one shall prostrate himself before You; all hearts shall fear You, and all innermost feelings and thoughts shall sing praises to Your name, as it is written, "All my bones shall say, 'Lord, who is like You? You save the poor man from one who is stronger than he, the poor and destitute from the one who would rob him'" (Psalms 35:10). Who is like You and who is equal to You and who can be compared to You, O great, strong, and awesome God, O highest power, Creator of the heavens and the earth. We shall praise and extol and glorify and bless Your holy name, as it is stated, " [A Psalm] of David. Bless the Lord, O my soul, and all *that is within me, His holy name" (Psalms 103:1). You are God, by virtue of Your strength; great, in the glory of Your name; strong forever; the Sovereign who sits on His high and elevated throne. He who dwells always; lofty and holy is His name. And as it is written, "Sing joyfully to the Lord, righteous ones; for the upright ones, praise is befitting" (Psalms 33:1). By the mouth of the upright shall You be praised; by the lips of the righteous shall You be blessed; by the tongue of the devout shall You be exalted; and among the holy shall You be sanctified.*

וּבְמַקְהֲלוֹת רִבְבוֹת עַמְּךָ בֵּית יִשְׂרָאֵל בְּרִנָּה יִתְפָּאֵר שִׁמְךָ, מַלְכֵּנוּ, בְּכָל דּוֹר וָדוֹר, שֶׁכֵּן חוֹבַת כָּל הַיְצוּרִים לְפָנֶיךָ, ה' אֱלֹהֵינוּ וֵאלֹהֵי אֲבוֹתֵינוּ, לְהוֹדוֹת לְהַלֵּל לְשַׁבֵּחַ, לְפָאֵר לְרוֹמֵם לְהַדֵּר לְבָרֵךְ, לְעַלֵּה וּלְקַלֵּס עַל כָּל דִּבְרֵי שִׁירוֹת וְתִשְׁבָּחוֹת דָּוִד בֶּן יִשַׁי עַבְדְּךָ מְשִׁיחֶךָ.

AND in the assemblies of the myriads of Your people, the House of Israel, in joyous song will Your name be glorified, our Sovereign, in each and every generation; for it is the duty of all creatures, before You, Lord our God and God of our ancestors, to thank, to praise, to extol, to glorify, to exalt, to lavish, to bless, to raise high, and to acclaim – beyond the words of the songs and praises of David, the son of Yishai, Your servant, Your anointed one.

יִשְׁתַּבַּח שִׁמְךָ לָעַד מַלְכֵּנוּ, הָאֵל הַמֶּלֶךְ הַגָּדוֹל וְהַקָּדוֹשׁ בַּשָּׁמַיִם וּבָאָרֶץ, כִּי לְךָ נָאֶה, ה' אֱלֹהֵינוּ וֵאלֹהֵי אֲבוֹתֵינוּ, שִׁיר וּשְׁבָחָה, הַלֵּל וְזִמְרָה, עֹז וּמֶמְשָׁלָה, נֶצַח, גְּדֻלָּה וּגְבוּרָה, תְּהִלָּה וְתִפְאֶרֶת, קְדֻשָּׁה וּמַלְכוּת, בְּרָכוֹת וְהוֹדָאוֹת מֵעַתָּה וְעַד עוֹלָם. בָּרוּךְ אַתָּה ה', אֵל מֶלֶךְ גָּדוֹל בַּתִּשְׁבָּחוֹת, אֵל הַהוֹדָאוֹת, אֲדוֹן הַנִּפְלָאוֹת, הַבּוֹחֵר בְּשִׁירֵי זִמְרָה, מֶלֶךְ אֵל חַי הָעוֹלָמִים.

MAY Your name be praised forever, our Sovereign, God, the great and holy Sovereign – in the heavens and in the earth. Because these are pleasing to You, O Lord our God and God of our ancestors: song and lauding, praise and hymn, boldness and dominion, triumph, greatness and strength, psalm and splendor, holiness and sovereignty, blessings and thanksgivings, from now and forever. Blessed are You, Lord, God, Sovereign, great in praise, God of thanksgiving, Master of wonders, who chooses the songs of hymn – Sovereign, God who gives life to the world.

אִלּוּ פִינוּ מָלֵא שִׁירָה כַיָּם
"Were our mouth as full of song as the sea..."

Klezmer Duo, Buenos Aires, Argentina, 2002

What does it mean to be "as full of song as the sea"?
What metaphor would you use to describe music based on this photograph?
What role does music play in your own spiritual life?

Scan here for further questions and texts relating to this photograph.

102

כוס רביעית
Kos Revi'it: Fourth Cup of Wine

בָּרוּךְ אַתָּה ה׳, אֱלֹהֵינוּ מֶלֶךְ הָעוֹלָם בּוֹרֵא פְּרִי הַגָּפֶן.

BLESSED are You, Lord our God, Sovereign of the universe, who creates the fruit of the vine.

וְשׁוֹתֶה בַּהֲסִבַּת שְׂמֹאל.

Drink while reclining to the left. Then recite the following:

בָּרוּךְ אַתָּה ה׳ אֱלֹהֵינוּ מֶלֶךְ הָעוֹלָם, עַל הַגֶּפֶן וְעַל פְּרִי הַגֶּפֶן, עַל תְּנוּבַת הַשָּׂדֶה וְעַל אֶרֶץ חֶמְדָּה טוֹבָה וּרְחָבָה שֶׁרָצִיתָ וְהִנְחַלְתָּ לַאֲבוֹתֵינוּ לֶאֱכוֹל מִפִּרְיָהּ וְלִשְׂבּוֹעַ מִטּוּבָהּ. רַחֶם נָא ה׳ אֱלֹהֵינוּ עַל יִשְׂרָאֵל עַמֶּךָ וְעַל יְרוּשָׁלַיִם עִירֶךָ וְעַל צִיּוֹן מִשְׁכַּן כְּבוֹדֶךָ וְעַל מִזְבְּחֶךָ וְעַל הֵיכָלֶךָ וּבְנֵה יְרוּשָׁלַיִם עִיר הַקֹּדֶשׁ בִּמְהֵרָה בְיָמֵינוּ וְהַעֲלֵנוּ לְתוֹכָהּ וְשַׂמְּחֵנוּ בְּבִנְיָנָהּ וְנֹאכַל מִפִּרְיָהּ וְנִשְׂבַּע מִטּוּבָהּ וּנְבָרֶכְךָ עָלֶיהָ בִּקְדֻשָּׁה וּבְטָהֳרָה [בשבת: וּרְצֵה וְהַחֲלִיצֵנוּ בְּיוֹם הַשַּׁבָּת הַזֶּה] וְשַׂמְּחֵנוּ בְּיוֹם חַג הַמַּצּוֹת הַזֶּה, כִּי אַתָּה ה׳ טוֹב וּמֵטִיב לַכֹּל, וְנוֹדֶה לְּךָ עַל הָאָרֶץ וְעַל פְּרִי הַגָּפֶן.

בָּרוּךְ אַתָּה ה׳, עַל הָאָרֶץ וְעַל פְּרִי הַגָּפֶן.

BLESSED are You, Lord our God, Sovereign of the universe, for the vine and for the fruit of the vine, and for the bounty of the field, and for a beloved, good, and expansive land, which You desired to give to our ancestors, to eat from its fruit and to be satiated from its goodness. Please have mercy, Lord our God, upon Israel Your people, and upon Jerusalem, Your city, and upon Zion, the dwelling place of Your glory, and upon Your altar, and upon Your sanctuary; and build Jerusalem Your holy city quickly in our days, and bring us into it and gladden us in its building, and we shall eat from its fruit, and be satiated from its goodness, and bless You in holiness and purity. [On Shabbat: And may You be pleased to enhance us on this Shabbat day] and gladden us on this day of the Festival of Matzot. for You, Lord, are good and do good to all; we thank You for the land and for the fruit of the vine.

BLESSED are You, Lord, for the land and for the fruit of the vine.

Seedlings, Kibbutz
Nir David, Israel,
1997

נִרְצָה
Nirtzah: Conclude

חֲסַל סִדּוּר פֶּסַח כְּהִלְכָתוֹ, כְּכָל מִשְׁפָּטוֹ וְחֻקָּתוֹ. כַּאֲשֶׁר זָכִינוּ לְסַדֵּר אוֹתוֹ כֵּן נִזְכֶּה לַעֲשׂוֹתוֹ. זָךְ שׁוֹכֵן מְעוֹנָה, קוֹמֵם קְהַל עֲדַת מִי מָנָה. בְּקָרוֹב נַהֵל נִטְעֵי כַנָּה פְּדוּיִים לְצִיּוֹן בְּרִנָּה.

לְשָׁנָה הַבָּאָה בִּירוּשָׁלַיִם הַבְּנוּיָה.

THE *Pesach Seder is concluded according to its laws, all its rules and statutes. Just as we have merited to prepare it, so too, may we merit its completion. Pure One who dwells in heaven, raise up this community from among Your countless assemblies. Quickly, lead the plantings of the sapling, redeemed, to Zion in joy.*

NEXT *year in the rebuilt Jerusalem!*

Next Year in Jerusalem!

L'shanah haba'ah bi'Yerushalayim – Next year in Jerusalem! With these three Hebrew (and four English) words, the official portion of the Passover Seder concludes. The final Yom Kippur service, Neilah, concludes in the same fashion. Twice each year, in spring and in fall, at high points of the Jewish liturgical calendar, Jews around the world echo one of the oldest traditions of the Jewish diaspora, expressing, in the words of Shulamit Elizur, "the hope of repeating the ceremony in Jerusalem in the following year and rejoicing in the rebuilding of the Temple" ("Ke-ha-yom ha-ze bi-Yerushalayim," *Tarbiz* 85:2 [2018]).

The phrase *"l'shanah haba'ah bi'Yerushalayim"* is both pregnant with meaning and ripe for interrogation. Who is responsible for returning Jews to Jerusalem – God or Jews themselves? Do Jews look forward to the rebuilding of the Temple as in ancient Jerusalem? To the peopling and upbuilding of present-day Jerusalem? Or to the heralding of a utopian future Jerusalem where peace and harmony reign supreme? For citizens of diaspora countries, does praying for an imminent return to Jerusalem square with the demands of patriotism and national loyalty?

As with so many of the questions Jews ask at the Passover Seder, no single answer suffices. Instead, systematic study of this three-word Hebrew phrase – its appearance, disappearance, translation, illustration, and interpretation – illuminates both the power of words in Jewish life and the power of Jerusalem, real and imagined, within Jewish culture.

The phrase *"l'shanah haba'ah bi'Yerushalayim"* provoked enormous anxiety in nineteenth- and twentieth-century Haggadot. Some discarded it, some left it untranslated, and some distorted its translation to protect the community's reputation. The history of the phrase's appearance, disappearance, translation, illustration, and interpretation testifies to its significance not only within the Haggadah but also within the larger religious, cultural, and political life of the Jew. "Next year in Jerusalem" echoes one of the oldest traditions of the Jewish diaspora and recalls centuries of ancestral longing. Yet it also reverberates with a question that seemingly every generation of diaspora Jews has pondered anew: What is my Jerusalem and where does it lie?

– **Prof. Jonathan D. Sarna**

ויהי בחצי הלילה

Va'yehi b'Chatzi Halailah: It Happened at Midnight

בליל ראשון אומרים:

On the first night say:

וּבְכֵן וַיְהִי בַּחֲצִי הַלָּיְלָה.

אָז רוֹב נִסִּים הִפְלֵאתָ בַּלַּיְלָה, בְּרֹאשׁ אַשְׁמוּרוֹת זֶה הַלָּיְלָה.

גֵּר צֶדֶק נִצַּחְתּוֹ כְּנֶחֱלַק לוֹ לַיְלָה, וַיְהִי בַּחֲצִי הַלָּיְלָה.

דַּנְתָּ מֶלֶךְ גְּרָר בַּחֲלוֹם הַלָּיְלָה, הִפְחַדְתָּ אֲרַמִּי בְּאֶמֶשׁ לַיְלָה.

וַיָּשַׂר יִשְׂרָאֵל לְמַלְאָךְ וַיּוּכַל לוֹ לַיְלָה, וַיְהִי בַּחֲצִי הַלָּיְלָה.

זֶרַע בְּכוֹרֵי פַתְרוֹס מָחַצְתָּ בַּחֲצִי הַלָּיְלָה, חֵילָם לֹא מָצְאוּ בְּקוּמָם בַּלַּיְלָה, טִיסַת נְגִיד חֲרֹשֶׁת סִלִּיתָ בְּכוֹכְבֵי לַיְלָה, וַיְהִי בַּחֲצִי הַלָּיְלָה.

יָעַץ מְחָרֵף לְנוֹפֵף אִוּוּי, הוֹבַשְׁתָּ פְגָרָיו בַּלַּיְלָה, כָּרַע בֵּל וּמַצָּבוֹ בְּאִישׁוֹן לַיְלָה, לְאִישׁ חֲמוּדוֹת נִגְלָה רָז חֲזוֹת לַיְלָה, וַיְהִי בַּחֲצִי הַלָּיְלָה.

מִשְׁתַּכֵּר בִּכְלֵי קֹדֶשׁ נֶהֱרַג בּוֹ בַּלַּיְלָה, נוֹשַׁע מִבּוֹר אֲרָיוֹת פּוֹתֵר בְּעִתּוּתֵי לָיְלָה, שִׂנְאָה נָטַר אֲגָגִי וְכָתַב סְפָרִים בַּלַּיְלָה, וַיְהִי בַּחֲצִי הַלָּיְלָה.

עוֹרַרְתָּ נִצְחֲךָ עָלָיו בְּנֶדֶד שְׁנַת לַיְלָה. פּוּרָה תִדְרוֹךְ לְשׁוֹמֵר מַה מִּלַּיְלָה, צָרַח כַּשׁוֹמֵר וְשָׂח אָתָא בֹקֶר וְגַם לַיְלָה, וַיְהִי בַּחֲצִי הַלָּיְלָה.

קָרֵב יוֹם אֲשֶׁר הוּא לֹא יוֹם וְלֹא לַיְלָה, רָם הוֹדַע כִּי לְךָ הַיּוֹם אַף לְךָ הַלָּיְלָה, שׁוֹמְרִים הַפְקֵד לְעִירְךָ כָּל הַיּוֹם וְכָל הַלַּיְלָה, תָּאִיר כְּאוֹר יוֹם חֶשְׁכַּת לַיְלָה, וַיְהִי בַּחֲצִי הַלָּיְלָה.

AND so, it happened at midnight.

THEN, most of the miracles did You wondrously happened at night, on the first watch of this night.

A righteous convert did You make victorious when it was divided at night [referring to Avraham in his war against the four kings, Genesis 14:15] – and it happened at midnight.

YOU judged the king of Gerrar in a dream in the night; you frightened an Aramean in the dark of the night; and Yisrael dominated an angel and was able to withstand Him at night [Genesis 32:25–30] – and it happened at midnight.

YOU crushed the firstborn of Patros [Pharaoh, as per Ezekiel 30:14]. in the middle of the night, their wealth they did not find when they got up at night; the attack of the leader Charoshet [Sisera] did you sweep away by the stars of the night [Judges 5:20] – and it happened at midnight.

WHEN the blasphemer [Sancheriv] counseled to attack, You struck his army at night [II Kings 19:35]; Bel and his pedestal were overturned in the pitch of night [in Nevuchadnezar's dream in Daniel 2]; to the man of delight [Daniel] was revealed the secret visions at night – and it happened at midnight.

THE one who got drunk [Balshatsar] from holy vessels was killed at night [Daniel 5:30]; the one saved from the pit of lions [Daniel] interpreted the scary visions of the night; hatred was harbored by the Agagite [Haman] when he wrote his edicts at night – and it happened at midnight.

YOU awakened victory upon him by disturbing his [Achashverosh's] sleep at night; You will stomp the wine press for the guards who ask, "What of the night?" [Esav/Seir, Isaiah 21:11]; He yelled like a guard and spoke: "The morning has come and also the night" – and it happened at midnight.

BRING close the day that is neither day nor night [referring to the end of days, Zechariah 14:7]; High One, make known that the day is Yours and also the night; appoint guards over Your city all day and all night; illuminate the darkness of the night as if it were the light of day – and it happened at midnight.

זבח פסח
Zevach Pesach: The Pesach Sacrifice

בליל שני בחו״ל:

On the second night (outside of Israel):

וּבְכֵן וַאֲמַרְתֶּם זֶבַח פֶּסַח.

אֹמֶץ גְּבוּרוֹתֶיךָ הִפְלֵאתָ בַּפֶּסַח, בְּרֹאשׁ כָּל מוֹעֲדוֹת נִשֵּׂאתָ פֶּסַח. גִּלִּיתָ לְאֶזְרָחִי חֲצוֹת לֵיל פֶּסַח, וַאֲמַרְתֶּם זֶבַח פֶּסַח.

דְּלָתָיו דָּפַקְתָּ כְּחֹם הַיּוֹם בַּפֶּסַח, הִסְעִיד נוֹצְצִים עֻגוֹת מַצּוֹת בַּפֶּסַח, וְאֶל הַבָּקָר רָץ זֵכֶר לְשׁוֹר עֵרֶךְ פֶּסַח, וַאֲמַרְתֶּם זֶבַח פֶּסַח.

זֹעֲמוּ סְדוֹמִים וְלוֹהֲטוּ בָּאֵשׁ בַּפֶּסַח, חֻלַּץ לוֹט מֵהֶם וּמַצּוֹת אָפָה בְּקֵץ פֶּסַח, טִאטֵאתָ אַדְמַת מוֹף וְנוֹף בְּעָבְרְךָ בַּפֶּסַח. וַאֲמַרְתֶּם זֶבַח פֶּסַח.

יָהּ רֹאשׁ כָּל הוֹן מָחַצְתָּ בְּלֵיל שִׁמּוּר פֶּסַח, כַּבִּיר, עַל בֵּן בְּכוֹר פָּסַחְתָּ בְּדַם פֶּסַח, לְבִלְתִּי תֵּת מַשְׁחִית לָבֹא בִּפְתָחַי בַּפֶּסַח, וַאֲמַרְתֶּם זֶבַח פֶּסַח.

מְסֻגֶּרֶת סֻגָּרָה בְּעִתּוֹתֵי פֶּסַח, נִשְׁמְדָה מִדְיָן בִּצְלִיל שְׂעוֹרֵי עֹמֶר פֶּסַח, שׂוֹרְפוּ מִשְׁמַנֵּי פּוּל וְלוּד בִּיקַד יְקוֹד פֶּסַח, וַאֲמַרְתֶּם זֶבַח פֶּסַח.

עוֹד הַיּוֹם בְּנֹב לַעֲמוֹד עַד גָּעָה עוֹנַת פֶּסַח, פַּס יַד כָּתְבָה לְקַעֲקֵעַ צוּל בַּפֶּסַח, צָפֹה הַצָּפִית עָרוֹךְ הַשֻּׁלְחָן בַּפֶּסַח, וַאֲמַרְתֶּם זֶבַח פֶּסַח.

קָהָל כִּנְּסָה הֲדַסָּה לְשַׁלֵּשׁ צוֹם בַּפֶּסַח, רֹאשׁ מִבֵּית רָשָׁע מָחַצְתָּ בְּעֵץ חֲמִשִּׁים בַּפֶּסַח, שְׁתֵּי אֵלֶּה רֶגַע תָּבִיא לְעוּצִית בַּפֶּסַח, תָּעֹז יָדְךָ תָּרוּם יְמִינְךָ כְּלֵיל הִתְקַדֵּשׁ חַג פֶּסַח, וַאֲמַרְתֶּם זֶבַח פֶּסַח.

AND so you shall say, "This is the Pesach sacrifice" (Exodus 12:27).

THE strength of Your heroic deeds did You wondrously show at Pesach; You raised Pesach up above of all the holidays; You made a revelation to the Ezrachite [Avraham] on Pesach night. And you shall say, "This is the Pesach sacrifice."

YOU knocked on his doors at the heat of the day on Pesach [Genesis 18:1]; he fed the angels cakes of matzah on Pesach; and he ran to the cattle in commemoration of the Pesach offering. And you shall say, "This is the Pesach sacrifice."

THE Sodomites angered You, and You set fire to them on Pesach; Lot was rescued from them, and he baked matzot at the end of Pesach; You swept the land of Mof and Nof [cities in Egypt] on Pesach. And you shall say, "This is the Pesach sacrifice."

YOU crushed the head of every firstborn [Egyptian] on the guarded night of Pesach; Powerful One, You passed over the firstborn son [of Israel] with the blood on Pesach; You would not let the destroyer come into my gates on Pesach. And you shall say, "This is the Pesach sacrifice."

THE walled city [of Jericho] fell in the season of Pesach; Midian was destroyed with a portion of barley like the omer on Pesach [Judges 7]; Pul and Lud [Assyrian soldiers] were burned in pyres on Pesach. And you shall say, "This is the Pesach sacrifice."

[SANCHERIV] remained in Nob [Isaiah 10:32] until the time of Pesach; the hand wrote [Daniel 5:5] of the destruction of the deep one [Balshatsar] on Pesach; the watch was set up and the table was set [referring to Balshatsar, based on Psalms 21:5] on Pesach. And you shall say, "This is the Pesach sacrifice."

HADASSAH assembled the people for a three-day fast on Pesach; You crushed the head of the house of evil [Haman] on a gallows fifty cubits high on Pesach; two [plagues, as per Isaiah 47:9] you will bring to the Utsi [Esav] on Pesach; strengthen Your hand, raise Your right arm, as on the night You were sanctified – the festival of Pesach. And you shall say, "This is the Pesach sacrifice."

כי לו נאה
Ki Lo Na'eh: For Him It Is Pleasant

כִּי לוֹ נָאֶה, כִּי לוֹ יָאֶה.

אַדִּיר בִּמְלוּכָה, בָּחוּר כַּהֲלָכָה, גְּדוּדָיו יֹאמְרוּ לוֹ: לְךָ וּלְךָ, לְךָ כִּי לְךָ, לְךָ אַף לְךָ, לְךָ ה' הַמַּמְלָכָה,
כִּי לוֹ נָאֶה, כִּי לוֹ יָאֶה.

דָּגוּל בִּמְלוּכָה, הָדוּר כַּהֲלָכָה, וָתִיקָיו יֹאמְרוּ לוֹ: לְךָ וּלְךָ, לְךָ כִּי לְךָ, לְךָ אַף לְךָ, לְךָ ה' הַמַּמְלָכָה,
כִּי לוֹ נָאֶה, כִּי לוֹ יָאֶה.

זַכַּאי בִּמְלוּכָה, חָסִין כַּהֲלָכָה טַפְסְרָיו יֹאמְרוּ לוֹ: לְךָ וּלְךָ, לְךָ כִּי לְךָ, לְךָ אַף לְךָ, לְךָ ה' הַמַּמְלָכָה,
כִּי לוֹ נָאֶה, כִּי לוֹ יָאֶה.

יָחִיד בִּמְלוּכָה, כַּבִּיר כַּהֲלָכָה לִמּוּדָיו יֹאמְרוּ לוֹ: לְךָ וּלְךָ, לְךָ כִּי לְךָ, לְךָ אַף לְךָ, לְךָ ה' הַמַּמְלָכָה,
כִּי לוֹ נָאֶה, כִּי לוֹ יָאֶה.

מוֹשֵׁל בִּמְלוּכָה, נוֹרָא כַּהֲלָכָה סְבִיבָיו יֹאמְרוּ לוֹ: לְךָ וּלְךָ, לְךָ כִּי לְךָ, לְךָ אַף לְךָ, לְךָ ה' הַמַּמְלָכָה,
כִּי לוֹ נָאֶה, כִּי לוֹ יָאֶה.

עָנָיו בִּמְלוּכָה, פּוֹדֶה כַּהֲלָכָה, צַדִּיקָיו יֹאמְרוּ לוֹ: לְךָ וּלְךָ, לְךָ כִּי לְךָ, לְךָ אַף לְךָ, לְךָ ה' הַמַּמְלָכָה,
כִּי לוֹ נָאֶה, כִּי לוֹ יָאֶה.

קָדוֹשׁ בִּמְלוּכָה, רַחוּם כַּהֲלָכָה שִׁנְאַנָּיו יֹאמְרוּ לוֹ: לְךָ וּלְךָ, לְךָ כִּי לְךָ, לְךָ אַף לְךָ, לְךָ ה' הַמַּמְלָכָה,
כִּי לוֹ נָאֶה, כִּי לוֹ יָאֶה.

תַּקִּיף בִּמְלוּכָה, תּוֹמֵךְ כַּהֲלָכָה תְּמִימָיו יֹאמְרוּ לוֹ: לְךָ וּלְךָ, לְךָ כִּי לְךָ, לְךָ אַף לְךָ, לְךָ ה' הַמַּמְלָכָה,
כִּי לוֹ נָאֶה, כִּי לוֹ יָאֶה.

Scan here and here to hear other popular tunes for the song.

While the Haggadah text remains virtually unchanged throughout the world, diverse communities bring their own customs and melodies to the Seder ritual. Scan here to hear how different Jewish communities sing "Ki Lo Na'eh."

FOR *Him it is pleasant, for Him it is suited.*

MIGHTY *in rulership, properly chosen, His troops shall say to Him, "To You – yes, to You, to You because it is Yours, to You and only You, to You, Lord, is the kingdom; for Him it is pleasant, for Him it is suited."*

NOTED *in rulership, properly splendid, His distinguished ones will say to Him, "To You – yes, to You, to You because it is Yours, to You and only You, to You, Lord, is the kingdom; for Him it is pleasant, for Him it is suited."*

MERITORIOUS *in rulership, properly robust, His scribes shall say to Him, "To You – yes, to You, to You because it is Yours, to You and only You, to You, Lord, is the kingdom; for Him it is pleasant, for Him it is suited."*

UNIQUE *in rulership, properly powerful, His wise ones say to Him, "To You – yes, to You, to You because it is Yours, to You and only You, to You, Lord, is the kingdom; for Him it is pleasant, for Him it is suited."*

GOVERNING *in rulership, properly awesome, those around Him say to Him, "To You – yes, to You, to You because it is Yours, to You and only You, to You, Lord, is the kingdom; for Him it is pleasant, for Him it is suited."*

HUMBLE *in rulership, properly restoring, His righteous ones say to Him, "To You – yes, to You, to You because it is Yours, to You and only You, to You, Lord, is the kingdom; for Him it is pleasant, for Him it is suited."*

HOLY *in rulership, properly merciful, His angels say to Him, "To You – yes, to You, to You because it is Yours, to You and only You, to You, Lord, is the kingdom; for Him it is pleasant, for Him it is suited."*

DYNAMIC *in rulership, properly supportive, His innocent ones say to Him, "To You – yes, to You, to You because it is Yours, to You and only You, to You, Lord, is the kingdom; for Him it is pleasant, for Him it is suited."*

אדיר הוא
Adir Hu: Mighty Is He

אַדִּיר הוּא יִבְנֶה בֵּיתוֹ בְּקָרוֹב. בִּמְהֵרָה, בִּמְהֵרָה, בְּיָמֵינוּ בְּקָרוֹב. אֵל בְּנֵה, אֵל בְּנֵה, בְּנֵה בֵּיתְךָ בְּקָרוֹב.

בָּחוּר הוּא, גָּדוֹל הוּא, דָּגוּל הוּא יִבְנֶה בֵּיתוֹ בְּקָרוֹב. בִּמְהֵרָה, בִּמְהֵרָה, בְּיָמֵינוּ בְּקָרוֹב. אֵל בְּנֵה, אֵל בְּנֵה, בְּנֵה בֵּיתְךָ בְּקָרוֹב.

הָדוּר הוּא, וָתִיק הוּא, זַכַּאי הוּא יִבְנֶה בֵּיתוֹ בְּקָרוֹב. בִּמְהֵרָה, בִּמְהֵרָה, בְּיָמֵינוּ בְּקָרוֹב. אֵל בְּנֵה, אֵל בְּנֵה, בְּנֵה בֵּיתְךָ בְּקָרוֹב.

חָסִיד הוּא, טָהוֹר הוּא, יָחִיד הוּא יִבְנֶה בֵּיתוֹ בְּקָרוֹב. בִּמְהֵרָה, בִּמְהֵרָה, בְּיָמֵינוּ בְּקָרוֹב. אֵל בְּנֵה, אֵל בְּנֵה, בְּנֵה בֵּיתְךָ בְּקָרוֹב.

כַּבִּיר הוּא, לָמוּד הוּא, מֶלֶךְ הוּא יִבְנֶה בֵּיתוֹ בְּקָרוֹב. בִּמְהֵרָה, בִּמְהֵרָה, בְּיָמֵינוּ בְּקָרוֹב. אֵל בְּנֵה, אֵל בְּנֵה, בְּנֵה בֵּיתְךָ בְּקָרוֹב.

נוֹרָא הוּא, סַגִּיב הוּא, עִזּוּז הוּא יִבְנֶה בֵּיתוֹ בְּקָרוֹב. בִּמְהֵרָה, בִּמְהֵרָה, בְּיָמֵינוּ בְּקָרוֹב. אֵל בְּנֵה, אֵל בְּנֵה, בְּנֵה בֵּיתְךָ בְּקָרוֹב.

פּוֹדֶה הוּא, צַדִּיק הוּא, קָדוֹשׁ הוּא יִבְנֶה בֵּיתוֹ בְּקָרוֹב. בִּמְהֵרָה, בִּמְהֵרָה, בְּיָמֵינוּ בְּקָרוֹב. אֵל בְּנֵה, אֵל בְּנֵה, בְּנֵה בֵּיתְךָ בְּקָרוֹב.

רַחוּם הוּא, שַׁדַּי הוּא, תַּקִּיף הוּא יִבְנֶה בֵּיתוֹ בְּקָרוֹב. בִּמְהֵרָה, בִּמְהֵרָה, בְּיָמֵינוּ בְּקָרוֹב. אֵל בְּנֵה, אֵל בְּנֵה, בְּנֵה בֵּיתְךָ בְּקָרוֹב.

Scan here to hear a popular tune for the song.

While the Haggadah text remains virtually unchanged throughout the world, diverse communities bring their own customs and melodies to the Seder ritual.
Scan here to hear how different Jewish communities sing "Adir Hu."

MIGHTY is He, may He build His house soon. Quickly, quickly, in our days, soon.

> God build, God build, build Your house soon.

CHOSEN is He, great is He, noted is He. Quickly, quickly, in our days, soon.

> God build, God build, build Your house soon.

SPLENDID is He, distinguished is He, meritorious is He. Quickly, quickly, in our days, soon.

> God build, God build, build Your house soon.

PIOUS is He, pure is He, unique is He. Quickly, quickly, in our days, soon.

> God build, God build, build Your house soon.

POWERFUL is He, wise is He, regal is He. Quickly, quickly, in our days, soon.

> God build, God build, build Your house soon.

AWESOME is He, exalted is He, heroic is He. Quickly, quickly, in our days, soon.

> God build, God build, build Your house soon.

A RESTORER is He, righteous is He, holy is He. Quickly, quickly, in our days, soon.

> God build, God build, build Your house soon.

MERCIFUL is He, the Omnipotent is He, dynamic is He. Quickly, quickly, in our days, soon.

> God build, God build, build Your house soon.

ספירת העומר
Sefirat Ha'Omer: Counting the Omer

ספירת העומר בחוץ לארץ, בליל שני של פסח:

Count the omer on the second night:

בָּרוּךְ אַתָּה ה׳, אֱלֹהֵינוּ מֶלֶךְ הָעוֹלָם, אֲשֶׁר קִדְּשָׁנוּ בְּמִצְוֹתָיו וְצִוָּנוּ עַל סְפִירַת הָעֹמֶר.
הַיּוֹם יוֹם אֶחָד בָּעֹמֶר.

BLESSED are You, Lord our God, Sovereign of the universe, who has sanctified us with His commandments and has commanded us to count the omer. Today is the first day of the omer.

*The Wall,
Jerusalem,
1992*

אחד מי יודע
ECHAD MI YODEA: WHO KNOWS ONE?

אֶחָד מִי יוֹדֵעַ? אֶחָד אֲנִי יוֹדֵעַ: אֶחָד אֱלֹהֵינוּ שֶׁבַּשָּׁמַיִם וּבָאָרֶץ.

שְׁנַיִם מִי יוֹדֵעַ? שְׁנַיִם אֲנִי יוֹדֵעַ: שְׁנֵי לֻחוֹת הַבְּרִית. אֶחָד אֱלֹהֵינוּ שֶׁבַּשָּׁמַיִם וּבָאָרֶץ.

שְׁלֹשָׁה מִי יוֹדֵעַ? שְׁלֹשָׁה אֲנִי יוֹדֵעַ: שְׁלֹשָׁה אָבוֹת, שְׁנֵי לֻחוֹת הַבְּרִית, אֶחָד אֱלֹהֵינוּ שֶׁבַּשָּׁמַיִם וּבָאָרֶץ.

אַרְבַּע מִי יוֹדֵעַ? אַרְבַּע אֲנִי יוֹדֵעַ: אַרְבַּע אִמָּהוֹת, שְׁלֹשָׁה אָבוֹת, שְׁנֵי לֻחוֹת הַבְּרִית, אֶחָד אֱלֹהֵינוּ שֶׁבַּשָּׁמַיִם וּבָאָרֶץ.

חֲמִשָּׁה מִי יוֹדֵעַ? חֲמִשָּׁה אֲנִי יוֹדֵעַ: חֲמִשָּׁה חוּמְשֵׁי תוֹרָה, אַרְבַּע אִמָּהוֹת, שְׁלֹשָׁה אָבוֹת, שְׁנֵי לֻחוֹת הַבְּרִית, אֶחָד אֱלֹהֵינוּ שֶׁבַּשָּׁמַיִם וּבָאָרֶץ.

שִׁשָּׁה מִי יוֹדֵעַ? שִׁשָּׁה אֲנִי יוֹדֵעַ: שִׁשָּׁה סִדְרֵי מִשְׁנָה, חֲמִשָּׁה חוּמְשֵׁי תוֹרָה, אַרְבַּע אִמָּהוֹת, שְׁלֹשָׁה אָבוֹת, שְׁנֵי לֻחוֹת הַבְּרִית, אֶחָד אֱלֹהֵינוּ שֶׁבַּשָּׁמַיִם וּבָאָרֶץ.

שִׁבְעָה מִי יוֹדֵעַ? שִׁבְעָה אֲנִי יוֹדֵעַ: שִׁבְעָה יְמֵי שַׁבַּתָּא, שִׁשָּׁה סִדְרֵי מִשְׁנָה, חֲמִשָּׁה חוּמְשֵׁי תוֹרָה, אַרְבַּע אִמָּהוֹת, שְׁלֹשָׁה אָבוֹת, שְׁנֵי לֻחוֹת הַבְּרִית, אֶחָד אֱלֹהֵינוּ שֶׁבַּשָּׁמַיִם וּבָאָרֶץ.

שְׁמוֹנָה מִי יוֹדֵעַ? שְׁמוֹנָה אֲנִי יוֹדֵעַ: שְׁמוֹנָה יְמֵי מִילָה, שִׁבְעָה יְמֵי שַׁבַּתָּא, שִׁשָּׁה סִדְרֵי מִשְׁנָה, חֲמִשָּׁה חוּמְשֵׁי תוֹרָה, אַרְבַּע אִמָּהוֹת, שְׁלֹשָׁה אָבוֹת, שְׁנֵי לֻחוֹת הַבְּרִית, אֶחָד אֱלֹהֵינוּ שֶׁבַּשָּׁמַיִם וּבָאָרֶץ.

תִּשְׁעָה מִי יוֹדֵעַ? תִּשְׁעָה אֲנִי יוֹדֵעַ: תִּשְׁעָה יַרְחֵי לֵדָה, שְׁמוֹנָה יְמֵי מִילָה, שִׁבְעָה יְמֵי שַׁבַּתָּא, שִׁשָּׁה סִדְרֵי מִשְׁנָה, חֲמִשָּׁה חוּמְשֵׁי תוֹרָה, אַרְבַּע אִמָּהוֹת, שְׁלֹשָׁה אָבוֹת, שְׁנֵי לֻחוֹת הַבְּרִית, אֶחָד אֱלֹהֵינוּ שֶׁבַּשָּׁמַיִם וּבָאָרֶץ.

עֲשָׂרָה מִי יוֹדֵעַ? עֲשָׂרָה אֲנִי יוֹדֵעַ: עֲשָׂרָה דִּבְּרַיָּא, תִּשְׁעָה יַרְחֵי לֵדָה, שְׁמוֹנָה יְמֵי מִילָה, שִׁבְעָה יְמֵי שַׁבַּתָּא, שִׁשָּׁה סִדְרֵי מִשְׁנָה, חֲמִשָּׁה חוּמְשֵׁי תוֹרָה, אַרְבַּע אִמָּהוֹת, שְׁלֹשָׁה אָבוֹת, שְׁנֵי לֻחוֹת הַבְּרִית, אֶחָד אֱלֹהֵינוּ שֶׁבַּשָּׁמַיִם וּבָאָרֶץ.

Synagogue Attic, Riga, Latvia, 1991

אֶחָד עֶשֶׂר מִי יוֹדֵעַ? אֶחָד עֶשֶׂר אֲנִי יוֹדֵעַ: אַחַד עֶשֶׂר כּוֹכְבַיָּא, עֲשָׂרָה דִּבְּרַיָּא, תִּשְׁעָה יַרְחֵי לֵדָה, שְׁמוֹנָה יְמֵי מִילָה, שִׁבְעָה יְמֵי שַׁבַּתָּא, שִׁשָּׁה סִדְרֵי מִשְׁנָה, חֲמִשָּׁה חוּמְשֵׁי תוֹרָה, אַרְבַּע אִמָּהוֹת, שְׁלֹשָׁה אָבוֹת, שְׁנֵי לֻחוֹת הַבְּרִית, אֶחָד אֱלֹהֵינוּ שֶׁבַּשָּׁמַיִם וּבָאָרֶץ.

שְׁנֵים עֶשֶׂר מִי יוֹדֵעַ? שְׁנֵים עֶשֶׂר אֲנִי יוֹדֵעַ: שְׁנֵים עֶשֶׂר שִׁבְטַיָּא, אַחַד עֶשֶׂר כּוֹכְבַיָּא, עֲשָׂרָה דִּבְּרַיָּא, תִּשְׁעָה יַרְחֵי לֵדָה, שְׁמוֹנָה יְמֵי מִילָה, שִׁבְעָה יְמֵי שַׁבַּתָּא, שִׁשָּׁה סִדְרֵי מִשְׁנָה, חֲמִשָּׁה חוּמְשֵׁי תוֹרָה, אַרְבַּע אִמָּהוֹת, שְׁלֹשָׁה אָבוֹת, שְׁנֵי לֻחוֹת הַבְּרִית, אֶחָד אֱלֹהֵינוּ שֶׁבַּשָּׁמַיִם וּבָאָרֶץ.

שְׁלֹשָׁה עֶשֶׂר מִי יוֹדֵעַ? שְׁלֹשָׁה עֶשֶׂר אֲנִי יוֹדֵעַ: שְׁלֹשָׁה עֶשֶׂר מִדַּיָּא, שְׁנֵים עֶשֶׂר שִׁבְטַיָּא, אַחַד עֶשֶׂר כּוֹכְבַיָּא, עֲשָׂרָה דִּבְּרַיָּא, תִּשְׁעָה יַרְחֵי לֵדָה, שְׁמוֹנָה יְמֵי מִילָה, שִׁבְעָה יְמֵי שַׁבַּתָּא, שִׁשָּׁה סִדְרֵי מִשְׁנָה, חֲמִשָּׁה חוּמְשֵׁי תוֹרָה, אַרְבַּע אִמָּהוֹת, שְׁלֹשָׁה אָבוֹת, שְׁנֵי לֻחוֹת הַבְּרִית, אֶחָד אֱלֹהֵינוּ שֶׁבַּשָּׁמַיִם וּבָאָרֶץ.

 While the Haggadah text remains virtually unchanged throughout the world, diverse communities bring their own customs and melodies to the Seder ritual. Scan here to hear how different Jewish communities sing "Echad Mi Yodea."

Scan here to hear a popular tune for the song.

WHO knows one? I know one: one is our God in the heavens and the earth.

WHO knows two? I know two: two are the tablets of the covenant, one is our God in the heavens and the earth.

WHO knows three? I know three: three are the fathers, two are the tablets of the covenant, one is our God in the heavens and the earth.

WHO knows four? I know four: four are the mothers, three are the fathers, two are the tablets of the covenant, one is our God in the heavens and the earth.

WHO knows five? I know five: five are the books of the Torah, four are the mothers, three are the fathers, two are the tablets of the covenant, one is our God in the heavens and the earth.

WHO knows six? I know six: six are the orders of the Mishnah, five are the books of the Torah, four are the mothers, three are the fathers, two are the tablets of the covenant, one is our God in the heavens and the earth.

WHO *knows seven? I know seven: seven are the days of the week, six are the orders of the Mishnah, five are the books of the Torah, four are the mothers, three are the fathers, two are the tablets of the covenant, one is our God in the heavens and the earth.*

WHO *knows eight? I know eight: eight are the days of circumcision, seven are the days of the week, six are the orders of the Mishnah, five are the books of the Torah, four are the mothers, three are the fathers, two are the tablets of the covenant, one is our God in the heavens and the earth.*

WHO *knows nine? I know nine: nine are the months of childbirth, eight are the days of circumcision, seven are the days of the week, six are the orders of the Mishnah, five are the books of the Torah, four are the mothers, three are the fathers, two are the tablets of the covenant, one is our God in the heavens and the earth.*

WHO *knows ten? I know ten: ten are the commandments, nine are the months of childbirth, eight are the days of circumcision, seven are the days of the week, six are the orders of the Mishnah, five are the books of the Torah, four are the mothers, three are the fathers, two are the tablets of the covenant, one is our God in the heavens and the earth.*

WHO *knows eleven? I know eleven: eleven are the stars [in Joseph's dream], ten are the commandments, nine are the months of childbirth, eight are the days of circumcision, seven are the days of the week, six are the orders of the Mishnah, five are the books of the Torah, four are the mothers, three are the fathers, two are the tablets of the covenant, one is our God in the heavens and the earth.*

WHO *knows twelve? I know twelve: twelve are the tribes, eleven are the stars [in Joseph's dream], ten are the commandments, nine are the months of childbirth, eight are the days of circumcision, seven are the days of the week, six are the orders of the Mishnah, five are the books of the Torah, four are the mothers, three are the fathers, two are the tablets of the covenant, one is our God in the heavens and the earth.*

WHO *knows thirteen? I know thirteen: thirteen are God's attributes, twelve are the tribes, eleven are the stars [in Joseph's dream], ten are the commandments, nine are the months of childbirth, eight are the days of circumcision, seven are the days of the week, six are the orders of the Mishnah, five are the books of the Torah, four are the mothers, three are the fathers, two are the tablets of the covenant, one is our God in the heavens and the earth.*

חד גדיא
Chad Gadya: One Kid

Shepherd, Kfar Zetim, Israel, 1984

חַד גַּדְיָא, חַד גַּדְיָא דְּזַבִּין אַבָּא בִּתְרֵי זוּזֵי, חַד גַּדְיָא, חַד גַּדְיָא.

וְאָתָא שׁוּנְרָא וְאָכְלָה לְגַדְיָא, דְּזַבִּין אַבָּא בִּתְרֵי זוּזֵי. חַד גַּדְיָא, חַד גַּדְיָא.

וְאָתָא כַּלְבָּא וְנָשַׁךְ לְשׁוּנְרָא, דְּאָכְלָה לְגַדְיָא, דְּזַבִּין אַבָּא בִּתְרֵי זוּזֵי. חַד גַּדְיָא, חַד גַּדְיָא.

וְאָתָא חוּטְרָא וְהִכָּה לְכַלְבָּא, דְּנָשַׁךְ לְשׁוּנְרָא, דְּאָכְלָה לְגַדְיָא, דְּזַבִּין אַבָּא בִּתְרֵי זוּזֵי. חַד גַּדְיָא, חַד גַּדְיָא.

וְאָתָא נוּרָא וְשָׂרַף לְחוּטְרָא, דְּהִכָּה לְכַלְבָּא, דְּנָשַׁךְ לְשׁוּנְרָא, דְּאָכְלָה לְגַדְיָא, דְּזַבִּין אַבָּא בִּתְרֵי זוּזֵי. חַד גַּדְיָא, חַד גַּדְיָא.

וְאָתָא מַיָּא וְכָבָה לְנוּרָא, דְּשָׂרַף לְחוּטְרָא, דְּהִכָּה לְכַלְבָּא, דְּנָשַׁךְ לְשׁוּנְרָא, דְּאָכְלָה לְגַדְיָא, דְּזַבִּין אַבָּא בִּתְרֵי זוּזֵי. חַד גַּדְיָא, חַד גַּדְיָא.

וְאָתָא תוֹרָא וְשָׁתָה לְמַיָּא, דְּכָבָה לְנוּרָא, דְּשָׂרַף לְחוּטְרָא, דְּהִכָּה לְכַלְבָּא, דְּנָשַׁךְ לְשׁוּנְרָא, דְּאָכְלָה לְגַדְיָא, דְּזַבִּין אַבָּא בִּתְרֵי זוּזֵי. חַד גַּדְיָא, חַד גַּדְיָא.

וְאָתָא הַשּׁוֹחֵט וְשָׁחַט לְתוֹרָא, דְּשָׁתָה לְמַיָּא, דְּכָבָה לְנוּרָא, דְּשָׂרַף לְחוּטְרָא, דְּהִכָּה לְכַלְבָּא, דְּנָשַׁךְ לְשׁוּנְרָא, דְּאָכְלָה לְגַדְיָא, דְּזַבִּין אַבָּא בִּתְרֵי זוּזֵי. חַד גַּדְיָא, חַד גַּדְיָא.

וְאָתָא מַלְאַךְ הַמָּוֶת וְשָׁחַט לְשׁוֹחֵט, דְּשָׁחַט לְתוֹרָא, דְּשָׁתָה לְמַיָּא, דְּכָבָה לְנוּרָא, דְּשָׂרַף לְחוּטְרָא, דְּהִכָּה לְכַלְבָּא, דְּנָשַׁךְ לְשׁוּנְרָא, דְּאָכְלָה לְגַדְיָא, דְּזַבִּין אַבָּא בִּתְרֵי זוּזֵי. חַד גַּדְיָא, חַד גַּדְיָא.

וְאָתָא הַקָּדוֹשׁ בָּרוּךְ הוּא וְשָׁחַט לְמַלְאַךְ הַמָּוֶת, דְּשָׁחַט לְשׁוֹחֵט, דְּשָׁחַט לְתוֹרָא, דְּשָׁתָה לְמַיָּא, דְּכָבָה לְנוּרָא, דְּשָׂרַף לְחוּטְרָא, דְּהִכָּה לְכַלְבָּא, דְּנָשַׁךְ לְשׁוּנְרָא, דְּאָכְלָה לְגַדְיָא, דְּזַבִּין אַבָּא בִּתְרֵי זוּזֵי. חַד גַּדְיָא, חַד גַּדְיָא.

While the Haggadah text remains virtually unchanged throughout the world, diverse communities bring their own customs and melodies to the Seder ritual.
Scan here to hear how different Jewish communities sing "Chad Gadya."

Shochet, Rosh Ha'ayin,
Israel, 1983

ONE kid, one kid that my father bought for two zuz. One kid, one kid.

THEN came a cat and ate the kid that my father bought for two zuz. One kid, one kid.

THEN came a dog and bit the cat that ate the kid that my father bought for two zuz. One kid, one kid.

THEN came a stick and hit the dog that bit the cat that ate the kid that my father bought for two zuz. One kid, one kid.

THEN came fire and burned the stick that hit the dog that bit the cat that ate the kid that my father bought for two zuz. One kid, one kid.

THEN came water and extinguished the fire that burned the stick that hit the dog that bit the cat that ate the kid that my father bought for two zuz. One kid, one kid.

THEN came a bull and drank the water that extinguished the fire that burned the stick that hit the dog that bit the cat that ate the kid that my father bought for two zuz. One kid, one kid.

THEN came the shochet and slaughtered the bull that drank the water that extinguished the fire that burned the stick that hit the dog that bit the cat that ate the kid that my father bought for two zuz. One kid, one kid.

THEN came the angel of death and slaughtered the shochet who slaughtered the bull that drank the water that extinguished the fire that burned the stick that hit the dog that bit the cat that ate the kid that my father bought for two zuz. One kid, one kid.

THEN came the Holy One, blessed be He, and slaughtered the angel of death, who slaughtered the schochet who slaughtered the bull that drank the water that extinguished the fire that burned the stick that hit the dog that bit the cat that ate the kid that my father bought for two zuz. One kid, one kid.

Twilight Mincha, Rosh
Ha'ayin, Israel, 1984

About the Photographer

Zion Ozeri

Born in Israel to immigrants from Yemen and currently living in New York City, Zion Ozeri is one of the world's leading photographers exploring the Jewish experience. Raised in Israel during a period of mass immigration, he interacted with many diverse cultures. This unique background gives him a cross-cultural perspective that suffuses his work.

Ozeri graduated from the Fashion Institute of Technology and Pratt Institute, both in New York City. His photographs have appeared in many national publications and have been exhibited in museums and galleries around the world. Ozeri has published several books, including *The Jewish World Family Haggadah* (New York: Simon and Schuster, 2005) and a coffee table book titled *The Jews of Yemen: The Last Generation* (Jerusalem: Keter, 2005).

He won a Simon Rockower Award for Excellence in Jewish Journalism in 2004 and is the recipient of the Covenant Award for 2013.

Ozeri founded the Jewish Lens curriculum and project in 2004, now being offered through ANU – Museum of the Jewish People in Israel. In addition, Ozeri founded and is the creative director of the early childhood project Within the Image, as well as DiverCity Lens, a curriculum and program implemented since 2010 in New York City public schools through the New York City Department of Education.

www.ZionOzeri.com   www.JewishLens.org   www.DiverCityLens.org   www.withinTheImage.org

About the Photographs

Sacred Passages, Rehovot, Israel, 1982

A Yemenite grandfather and his grandson study the weekly Torah portion together outside their small hut in the Israeli city of Rehovot.

Four Mothers, Mevaseret Zion Absorption Center, Israel, 2000

Often framed as a monolithic society, Israel is in fact made up of the many stories of the immigrating families who have built their lives there, united under the values of a shared heritage and history. The reality for new arrivals to Israel is often harsher than the promised dream of "a land flowing with milk and honey." These challenges are a reminder of the complexity of building a singular nation that comprises immigrants from every corner of the earth.

The Arlene Fern School, Buenos Aires, Argentina, 2002

On July 18, 1994, a terrorist bombing at the AMIA (Argentine Israelite Mutual Association) in Buenos Aires killed eighty-five people and injured hundreds more. The deadliest terrorist attack in Argentina's history, the bombing rocked the country's Jewish community of more than 200,000. Feeling a need to counter that destruction with something positive and productive, the community founded the Arlene Fern Community School in 1995. The school serves more than five hundred students in the primary grades.

Holiday Lights, Mumbai, India, 2001

The woman in this photograph is lighting hanging oil lamps in honor of the holiday of Purim. Although Jewish law doesn't require the kindling of lights for Purim, it is the tradition in her community to welcome all holidays with light. She is part of India's B'nei Yisrael community, the largest Jewish community remaining in the country. According to tradition, the original members of the B'nei Yisrael were shipwrecked on the Indian coast more than two thousand years ago, and they've been there ever since. Although the community is smaller today than it once was, it still strives to preserve its Jewish identity, its connection to Israel, and its unique local customs.

Wine Making, Tashkent, Uzbekistan, 1998

A Jewish woman separates the grapes from the stems as she prepares to begin the wine-making process outside her home in Tashkent, Uzbekistan.

Synagogue, Alibag, India, 2001

The caretaker of the Magen Avot Synagogue in Alibag, India, and his brother kiss the building's massive mezuzah as they give the photographer a tour of the facility. The synagogue was founded in 1840, and the current building dates to 1910.

Soup Kitchen, Buenos Aires, Argentina, 2002

This soup kitchen in Buenos Aires is run by the American Joint Distribution Committee, a global humanitarian organization that assists Jewish communities throughout the world. Established during World War I, the JDC continues to provide aid and relief for communities in crisis and supports programs that help sustain Jewish communal life worldwide.

Farmer, Eastern Galilee, Israel, 1987

The Galilee, in northern Israel, is the country's most fertile agricultural region. It is also known for its beautiful rolling hills and valleys.

Soup Kitchen, New York City, New York, 1992

A homeless man exits a synagogue in Lower Manhattan after receiving a meal at the shul's soup kitchen. The soup kitchen serves all who are hungry — whether they're Jewish or not.

Kitchen, Kiev, Ukraine, 1991

Jews have lived in Ukraine since at least the eighth century and were one of the country's largest minority groups by the seventeenth century. Although a center for Jewish life and learning, Ukraine was also the site of some of history's most virulent pogroms and antisemitic attacks. More than a million Jews were killed in Ukraine during World War II, and many Ukrainian Jews have subsequently moved to Israel – yet the European nation is still home to the fifth-largest Jewish population in the world. Recent decades have seen a revival of Jewish life in Ukraine, with renewed interest in Jewish tradition and observance and newly reimagined Jewish institutions.

Brooklyn, USA, 1996

Two young students look up admiringly at their teacher in a yeshiva in Brooklyn. Behind his back, he holds a Hebrew language primer – perhaps the day's lesson.

Cave, Haidan, Northern Yemen, 1992

Making best use of the limited space available to them, these boys have gathered in a cave in a rugged and mountainous part of Yemen to study the weekly Torah portion. Jews have lived in Yemen since ancient times, though they've generally been treated as second-class citizens by the Muslim authorities. Aliyah from Yemen began in the late 1880s, culminating in 1949–50 with a huge airlift known as Operation Magic Carpet. For the Yemenite Jews, this airlift seemed to fulfill Isaiah's prophecy that the Jewish people would be brought to the promised land "on the wings of eagles." Today, only a tiny Jewish population remains in Yemen.

Let My People Go, New York City, USA, 1987

At a demonstration in New York City, Jews rally for the release of their Soviet brothers and sisters. Under Soviet rule, Jews weren't allowed to practice their religion or immigrate to Israel or America. In solidarity, American Jews held demonstrations, petitioned the US government to pressure the Soviets, and even smuggled Jewish books and religious objects into the USSR. By the end of the 1980s, political shifts and economic collapse in the Soviet Union, along with pressure from the world Jewish community, radically altered the landscape for Soviet Jews. Within a few years, hundreds of thousands of Jews were allowed to leave the USSR and begin new lives in the United States and Israel.

Honorable Discharge, Ben Gurion Airport, Israel, 1992

This man is one of the hundreds of thousands of Jews from the former Soviet Union who flocked to Israel after Gorbachev opened the doors to emigration in 1989. Here is how the photographer, Zion Ozeri, describes the photograph: "I call it *Honorable Discharge*. He was obviously discharged from the Russian army. And many Jews either sacrificed their lives or fought heroically during World War II. I always look for the image that will define the moment, so to speak. And I saw it in his face. You see the flag, you see El Al, and that look."

Study Group, Seattle, Washington, USA, 2009

Whether in a cave in rural Yemen or a synagogue library in Seattle, text study is central to the Jewish experience. Here, the intent expressions on the faces and the pile of open books at the center of the table attest to the seriousness with which these participants approach their learning. This photograph is reproduced, with permission, from the book *A Covenant of Dreams* (Covenant Foundation, 2009).

Sunrise Shema, Sde Boker Israel, 2003

In the heart of the Negev Desert, just outside Kibbutz Sde Boker, a small group gathers for a sunrise Shacharit prayer service. In 1953, Israel's first prime minister, David Ben-Gurion, retired to Sde Boker, hoping to inspire more Israelis to move to the Negev and make the barren land flourish. Over the decades since, Israel has built dozens of new cities, towns, and kibbutzim in the desert, helping to fulfill Ben-Gurion's dream.

Nursery School, Santiago, Chile, 2002

Chile is home to the third-largest Jewish community in South America, with the majority of the country's eighteen thousand Jews living in the capital of Santiago. Although the first Jews arrived in Chile with the Spanish conquistadors, significant Jewish immigration from Europe did not begin until the mid-nineteenth century.

The Secret, Mevaseret Zion Absorption Center, Israel, 1990

These two boys – one from Ethiopia, one from the former Soviet Union – have met in a kindergarten class at an absorption center near Jerusalem. Absorption centers provide temporary housing and an introduction to Israeli life for many new immigrants. Ozeri notes, "The absorption center is something I don't think they have anywhere else in the world. It's a place where you can ease yourself into your new home. They help initiate you into a new life in Israel and how to deal with everyday things from the very, very simple – like shopping in the supermarket – to finding a job."

Blessings for the Circumcised, Mexico City, Mexico, 2004

In the book of Genesis, God instructs Abraham to circumcise himself and his male descendants as a sign of their covenant with God. Throughout Jewish history, this ritual circumcision (*brit milah* in Hebrew) has remained a core Jewish practice and symbol of identity, linking generations across time and space.

Bookcase, Plovdiv, Bulgaria, 2000

The Plovdiv Synagogue has been around for centuries; today, it is one of just two synagogues still in use in Bulgaria. The current building was constructed in the 1880s and restored in 2003.

Tourists, Negev, Israel, 2005

The Negev in southern Israel is more than just a desert. From Eilat in the south to Mitzpeh Ramon, Sde Boker, and the city of Be'er Sheva, the Negev offers a variety of attractions for tourists, including beaches, nature, archaeology, history, and of course, camel rides.

Summer Camp, Tumwater, Washington, USA, 2002

It's time for morning services at Camp Solomon Schechter, in Tumwater, Washington. As the Torah is raised, the campers point with their fingers, symbolically kissing the Torah and lending their support to the *magbiah*, the one who lifts up the scroll.

Oil Pressers, Alibag, India, 2001

This Jewish family lives in Alibag, India, a village outside of Mumbai. Many of the Jews from the towns and villages around Mumbai have worked as oil pressers for generations. In fact, they were known among their non-Jewish neighbors as Shanwar Telis, or "Saturday Oil Pressers," because they didn't work on Shabbat. In this picture, you can see some symbols of Jewish life – like the Magen David (Jewish star) and Hamsa (good-luck sign in the shape of a hand) – alongside the traditional tools of the oil pressers' trade.

Outdoor Market, Samarkand, Uzbekistan, 1998

Central Asia – comprising portions of modern Uzbekistan, Tajikistan, and Kyrgyzstan – is home to one of the world's oldest Jewish communities. Some Bukharan Jews, as they are known, trace their lineage back to the lost tribes of Israel; others place their origins within the reign of Persian King Cyrus the Great in the sixth century BCE. Over the centuries, their relative isolation from mainstream Judaism has led to the development of a unique and distinctive Central Asian Jewish culture.

Palmachim Beach, Israel, 2002

A national park as well as a tourist spot, Palmachim Beach on Israel's central Mediterranean coast is named for the Palmach (short for Plugot Machatz, literally, "strike forces") – an elite unit of the underground Jewish army in pre-state Palestine.

Jewish Quarter, Jerusalem, Israel, 1984

Beyond the row of hanging *tzitziot* (fringes) in this photograph, just below the Muslim holy site known as the Dome of the Rock, you can spot the single arch of the Churva (Ruin) Synagogue. An important center for Jewish life in the nineteenth century, the synagogue was destroyed by the Jordanians when they captured Jerusalem in 1948. After retaking the Old City in 1967, Israeli authorities left the remains of the ruined synagogue intact, rebuilding just one of its arches as a reminder of its history. In 2010, the building was finally restored and is once again a center of Jewish life in the Old City.

Matzah Oven, Bukhara, Uzbekistan, 2000

An elderly woman removes a piece of freshly baked round matzah from a clay oven. Ozeri notes: "Even though they had access to factory-made matzot, many of the Jews in Bukhara preferred this hand-baked matzah — which, I have to say, was a much tastier matzah than anything we have here [in the United States]." This photograph, taken after the breakup of the Soviet Union, reflects a community in transition. The Jewish population in the city of Bukhara — once numbering more than twenty thousand — had already begun to shrink significantly with immigration to the United States and Israel. Today, large, vibrant communities in New York and Jerusalem carry on the ancestral traditions, while just a few hundred Jews still remain in the city of Bukhara.

Backpack, Operation Solomon, Ben Gurion Airport, Israel, 1991

In 1990, Israel and Ethiopia reached an agreement that would allow Ethiopia's remaining Jews to move to Israel. But before anything could be done, rebel forces threatened to topple the Ethiopian government. So in May 1991, as the rebels seized control of Ethiopia's capital, the Israeli government organized an unprecedented rescue operation, called Operation Solomon. Beginning on Friday, May 24, and continuing nonstop for a day and a half, El Al jumbo jets and military transport planes carried more than fourteen thousand Ethiopian Jews to freedom in Israel. The people in this photograph were part of Operation Solomon. The man carries his mother on his back as they enter the land of Israel for the first time. Look at the expressions on their faces. How do you think they feel?

Holocaust Survivor, Buenos Aires, Argentina, 2002

The central figure in this photograph, a Holocaust survivor who writes and lectures about his experiences, is pictured surrounded by his grandchildren. Ozeri explains: "I was concerned about taking a meaningful photograph of him. I could have taken his photograph sitting alone in a chair, but I decided that his dignity would shine through more if he was surrounded by his grandchildren. Holocaust survivors lost so much family and they didn't think they would have any future. This is showing that they really do."

Amiaz Plains, Israel, 2002

The dramatic hills and rock formations of the Amiaz Plains rise to the west of the Dead Sea, in Israel's Judaean Desert.

133

Wine Cellar, Djerba, Tunisia, 1995

A woman sits watch over a batch of freshly made wine in Djerba, Tunisia, to make sure it's not handled by non-Jewish hands – a traditional requirement for kosher wine. According to local lore, Jews first arrived on the Tunisian island of Djerba more than twenty-five hundred years ago, as members of the priestly class fleeing the destruction of Jerusalem at the hands of the Babylonians. To this day, Djerba has an unusually high percentage of Kohanim (descendants of the ancient priests). Despite numerous ups and downs over the course of its long history, Djerba's Jewish community of more than a thousand remains vibrant and active today.

Jewish Community Center, Detroit, USA, 2009

Most of the matzah we see today is of the square, machine-made variety. But matzah can really be any size or shape, as these children demonstrate at a matzah-making workshop at a JCC in Detroit. This photograph is reproduced, with permission, from the book *A Covenant of Dreams* (Covenant Foundation, 2009).

Sunset, Nahariya, Israel, 1995

This peaceful scene captures a quiet moment in the seaside town of Nahariya, in northern Israel. But the calm and contentment of the serene sunset is disturbed ever so slightly by the silhouette of the man's crutches, perhaps a small reminder of the violence and conflict that is a perennial aspect of Israeli life.

Setting the Table, Santiago de Cuba, Cuba, 2003

Members of Cuba's Jewish community in the city of Santiago set out refreshments for a conversion class. Jews have lived in Cuba for centuries; some believe the island's first Jews were Spanish conversos (secret Jews) who arrived in 1492 with Christopher Columbus. Cuba's Jewish population peaked at more than twenty thousand in the 1920s, but the vast majority fled to the US and Israel after the Revolution of 1959. Today, the community numbers only around five hundred.

New Immigrant, Lod, Israel, 1997

Israel is known for its succulent watermelons – and its adorable children.

134

Grace after Meal, Jewish Day School, Casablanca, Morocco, 2004

Although Jews have faced times of oppression during their long history in this Muslim nation, Morocco is today one of the most welcoming to Jews of all the nations of the Arab world. The country's constitution protects Jews as vital members of Moroccan society. The city of Casablanca is home to Morocco's largest Jewish population (about three thousand) and boasts a number of Jewish schools, old-age homes, synagogues, and restaurants.

Jewish Quarter, Jerusalem, Israel, 1995

The Old City of Jerusalem is a walled enclave of narrow alleys and stone buildings dating back many centuries. Until the nineteenth century, the Old City constituted the entire city of Jerusalem, but in modern times, the city has expanded well beyond the Old City walls. Today, the historic structures of the Old City stand in contrast to the bustling modern city that surrounds them.

Wine Cellar, Samarkand, Uzbekistan, 1998

This woman makes wine here in her cellar, in the Uzbek city of Samarkand. You can see the grapes she's hung up to dry, the pots in which she ferments the fruit, and the bottles into which she puts the finished product. For many years, Jews in Uzbekistan did not have access to kosher wine for Shabbat and holidays. So they had to make it themselves. Although today it is much easier to get kosher wine from Israel or the United States, some members of the dwindling community continue the tradition of making their own wine.

Elijah's Chair, Kokand, Uzbekistan, 1999

The prophet Elijah is a familiar guest at all Seders, believed to sip from the special goblet we set aside for him. But Elijah also traditionally attends every Jewish circumcision ceremony. A separate chair — often specially carved or decorated — is set aside at the bris for the prophet known as the "Angel of the Covenant."

Debbie Friedman, Aspen, Colorado, USA, 1996

From synagogues and summer camps to concert halls around the world, singer-songwriter Debbie Friedman inspired millions with her affirming Jewish folk compositions and contemporary adaptations of Jewish liturgy. Her songs, such as "Misheberach," "Lechi Lach," and "Not by Might," continue to introduce new generations of American Jews to the power of prayer and spirituality. Debbie Friedman died in 2011 at the age of fifty-nine.

Klezmer Duo, Buenos Aires, Argentina, 2002

The two men in this picture are from Buenos Aires, Argentina. Although the photo was taken at their music studio in Argentina, their klezmer band plays all over the world. Argentina is home to the largest Jewish community in Central and South America, though economic challenges have pushed many young Argentine Jews to emigrate to Israel and elsewhere in search of new opportunities.

Seedlings, Kibbutz Nir David, Israel, 1997

Located in the Beit She'an Valley of Northern Israel, Kibbutz Nir David was founded in 1936 as Tel Amal. It was renamed in the 1940s to honor David Wolfsohn, the second president of the World Zionist Organization. Today, the kibbutz is known for raising fish and a variety of agricultural products, and as home to Gan HaShlosha, a natural water park.

The Wall, Jerusalem, 1992

As the only remnant of the ancient Temple complex, the Western Wall (a retaining wall built by Herod the Great) has been a Jewish pilgrimage site for centuries. When Israel captured the Old City of Jerusalem in 1967, authorities built this large plaza on the site of the city's Moroccan Quarter to accommodate large numbers of visitors. The plaza can hold up to 400,000 tourists and worshippers on the busiest days.

Synagogue Attic, Riga, Latvia, 1991

Before World War II, there were many synagogues in Riga, the capital of Latvia. In fact, until the twentieth century, Eastern Europe was a center for Jewish life and learning. But today, only one synagogue still stands in Riga. Ozeri explains how he came to take this picture: "When we came, there were only a few elderly men in the synagogue. The one in the picture is the gabbai. I found it strange that in a big synagogue there were only a few prayer books. And I asked the translator to ask him about that. And the man got a little insulted, because he thought I was questioning their Jewishness. So he said to the translator, 'Does he want to see books? I'll show him books.' So he took us to the attic. It turns out they had put all of their books in the attic, because the Communists didn't want to see that richness of Jewish life. Because when you see so many books, what does that mean? It means that this culture and tradition is very rich."

Shepherd, Kfar Zeitim, Israel, 1984

A shepherd leads his children on a horse near Moshav Kfar Zeitim in northern Israel.

Shochet, Rosh Ha'ayin, Israel, 1983

The bloodstains on this man's shirt point to his profession: he's a shochet – a butcher who slaughters animals according to the laws of kashrut. He stands at the sink and checks his blade. In order for a land animal or bird to be kosher, it must be slaughtered with a single stoke across the neck from a perfectly sharpened knife. This ensures the most painless, humane death for the animal. After the animal is killed, the shochet lets the blood drain out to comply with the Torah's prohibition against consuming animal blood.

Twilight Mincha, Rosh Ha'ayin, Israel, 1984

Founded in 1949, the Central Israeli town of Rosh Ha'ayin became home to many of the Yemenite Jews who were airlifted to Israel in 1949 and 1950. The town of approximately sixty thousand still maintains a large Yemenite community.

About the Contributors

Joshua A. Feinberg, Writer and Educator

Joshua A. Feinberg, the content editor for this Haggadah, is an independent consultant specializing in content development and writing for museum exhibitions, media, and educational materials. After earning his master's degree in museum education from Bank Street College, Mr. Feinberg served for several years on the education staff of the Jewish Museum in New York. As an independent consultant, Mr. Feinberg has written audio tours, arts-based curricula, and exhibition content for a wide range of institutions, including the American Museum of Natural History, the National Museum of American Jewish History, the Ellis Island Museum, and the Metropolitan Museum of Art.

Sara Wolkenfeld, Chief Learning Officer, Sefaria

Rabbanit Sara Wolkenfeld, who served as an advisor to this project, is the Chief Learning Officer at Sefaria, an online database and interface for Jewish texts. She is passionate about expanding Jewish textual knowledge for all. Sara is also a fellow at the David Hartman Center at the Hartman Institute of North America. Her previous experience includes serving as Director of Education at the Center for Jewish Life – Hillel at Princeton University as part of the OU's Jewish Learning Initiative on Campus. She studied Talmud and Jewish law at various institutions of Jewish learning in Israel and America, including Midreshet Lindenbaum, Drisha, Nishmat, and Beit Morasha. She speaks on various Jewish topics at synagogues, schools, and university communities. Sara lives in Chicago with her husband and their five children.

Samantha Siegler, Art Historian and Photographer

Samantha Siegler, who contributed to the initial design concept of this Haggadah, is an art historian and photographer based in London and New York. She is currently pursuing graduate work at the Courtauld Institute of Art and previously earned a BA from Cornell University.

Rabbi Dr. Joshua Berman, Professor of Tanakh, Bar-Ilan University

A graduate of Princeton University, Rabbi Berman received his rabbinic ordination from the Chief Rabbinate of Israel after learning for eight years at Yeshivat Har-Etzion in Gush Etzion, Israel. He is the author of *The Temple: Its Symbolism and Meaning Then and Now* (Northvale, NJ: Jason Aronson, 1995), National Jewish Book Award finalist *Created Equal: How the Bible Broke with Ancient Political Thought* (Oxford, 2008), and *Inconsistency in the Torah: Ancient Literary Convention and the Limits of Source Criticism* (Oxford, 2017). His articles and essays have appeared in *Mosaic Magazine* and the *Wall Street Journal*. He, his wife, and their four children reside in Bet Shemesh, Israel.

Dr. Mijal Bitton, Rosh Kehilla and cofounder, Downtown Minyan, New York City

Dr. Mijal Bitton is a Scholar in Residence at the Shalom Hartman Institute of North America and the Rosh Kehilla (communal leader) and cofounder of the Downtown Minyan in New York City. Dr. Bitton received a BA from Yeshiva University and earned her doctorate from New York University, where she conducted an ethnographic study of a Syrian Jewish community, with a focus on developing the field of contemporary Sephardic studies in America. She is an alumna of the Wexner Graduate Fellowship. In 2018, Dr. Bitton was selected for inclusion in the New York *Jewish Week*'s "36 Under 36." She lives in Manhattan with her husband Sion and their two children.

Rabbi Daniel Bouskila, Director, Sephardic Educational Center; Rabbi, Westwood Village Synagogue, Los Angeles

Rabbi Daniel Bouskila is the Director of the Sephardic Educational Center (SEC), an international organization whose philosophy reflects classic Sephardic Judaism's creative blend of tradition and modernity. Under his leadership, the SEC has become a think tank that specializes in translating the moderate halachic approach and tolerant worldview of the major rabbinic personalities of the Sephardic tradition. Rabbi Bouskila is also the rabbi of the Westwood Village Synagogue (WVS), a vibrant and welcoming Modern Orthodox congregation in Los Angeles. He holds a BA in history from UCLA and rabbinic ordination from Yeshiva University. Rabbi Bouskila studied at Yeshivat Kerem B'Yavneh in Israel, served in the IDF's Givati Infantry Brigade, and studied S. Y. Agnon's literature at the Hebrew University in Jerusalem. He is a regular contributor to the *Jewish Journal* of Greater Los Angeles.

Rabbi Elliot J. Cosgrove, PhD, Rabbi,
Park Avenue Synagogue, New York City

Ordained at the Jewish Theological Seminary in 1999, Rabbi Cosgrove earned his PhD at the University of Chicago Divinity School and has been Rabbi of Park Avenue Synagogue in New York City since 2008. Rabbi Cosgrove is the author of twelve collections of selected sermons: *In the Beginning* (2009), *An Everlasting Covenant* (2010), *Go Forth!* (2011), *Hineni* (2012), *A Place to Lodge* (2013), *Living Waters* (2014), *Stairway to Heaven* (2015), *Rise Up!* (2016), *A Coat of Many Colors* (2017), *Provisions for the Way* (2018), *Tree of Life* (2019), and *Bring Them Close* (2020). He is the editor of *Jewish Theology in Our Time: A New Generation Explores the Foundations and Future of Jewish Belief.* His essays and op-eds appear frequently in a variety of Jewish publications, including the *Jewish Week* and the *Forward.*

Dr. Daniel Gordis, Senior Vice President and
Koret Distinguished Fellow, Shalem College

Dr. Daniel Gordis is Senior Vice President and Koret Distinguished Fellow at Shalem College in Jerusalem. The author of twelve books, Gordis is a regular columnist for *Bloomberg Opinion*. Gordis's history of Israel, *Israel: A Concise History of a Nation Reborn* (New York: Ecco, 2016), received the 2016 National Jewish Book Award as Book of the Year. Ambassador Dennis Ross, reflecting on the book, wrote, "When I am asked, 'Is there one book to read about Israel?' I now have an answer." Gordis's book *We Stand Divided: The Rift between American Jews and Israel* (Ecco) was published in 2019. Dr. Gordis and his wife live in Jerusalem.

Yossi Klein Halevi, Senior Fellow, Shalom Hartman Institute

Yossi Klein Halevi is a senior fellow at the Shalom Hartman Institute in Jerusalem. Together with Imam Abdullah Antepli of Duke University, he codirects the Institute's Muslim Leadership Initiative (MLI), which teaches emerging young Muslim American leaders about Judaism, Jewish identity, and Israel. Halevi's 2013 book *Like Dreamers* won the Jewish Book Council's Everett Book of the Year Award. His book *Letters to My Palestinian Neighbor* (New York: Harper, 2018) is a *New York Times* bestseller. He writes for leading op-ed pages in the United States, including the *New York Times* and the *Wall Street Journal*, and is a former contributing editor to the *New Republic.*

Rabbi Ammiel Hirsch, Senior Rabbi, Stephen
Wise Free Synagogue, New York City

Rabbi Ammiel Hirsch is the Senior Rabbi of Stephen Wise Free Synagogue in New York City, where he has led a dramatic revival in Jewish life introducing major changes in worship, ritual, and education, attracting a new generation. Rabbi Hirsch is recognized internationally for his leadership in Jewish affairs and is frequently cited in the media. In 2018, the *Jerusalem Post* named him among "The 50 Most Influential Jews of the Year." He is a recipient of numerous awards and sits on the boards of many international and national Jewish and interfaith organizations. An accomplished teacher and public speaker, Rabbi Hirsch is coauthor of the acclaimed *One People, Two Worlds: A Reform Rabbi and an Orthodox Rabbi Explore the Issues That Divide Them* (New York: Schocken, 2002). Rabbi Hirsch received his ordination at the Hebrew Union College-Jewish Institute of Religion in New York. He also received an LLB Honors (law degree) from the London School of Economics and is a member of the New York State Bar. From 1977 to 1980, Rabbi Hirsch served as a tank commander in the Israel Defense Forces.

Rabba Sara Hurwitz, President and
Cofounder, Yeshivat Maharat

Rabba Sara Hurwitz, President and Cofounder of Maharat, the first institution to ordain Orthodox women as clergy, also serves on the rabbinic staff of the Hebrew Institute of Riverdale. Rabba Hurwitz completed the three-year Scholars Circle Program at Drisha Institute, an advanced intensive program of study for Jewish women training to become scholars, educators, and community leaders. After an additional five years of study under the auspices of Rabbi Avi Weiss, she was ordained by Rabbi Weiss and Rabbi Daniel Sperber in 2009. Rabba Hurwitz has been named as one of the New York *Jewish Week*'s "36 Under 36," the *Forward*'s "Forward 50" most influential Jewish leaders, and *Newsweek*'s "50 Most Influential Rabbis in America." In 2017, Rabba Hurwitz was selected as a member of the inaugural class of Wexner Foundation Field Fellows.

Prof. Deborah E. Lipstadt, PhD, Dorot Professor of Modern
Jewish History and Holocaust Studies, Emory University

Deborah Lipstadt is Dorot Professor of Modern Jewish History and Holocaust Studies at Emory University in Atlanta, Georgia. She is perhaps best known for having been sued for libel by David Irving, one of the world's leading Holocaust deniers. The case, which lasted for six years, resulted in the court declaring Irving to be "a right-wing polemicist," who engages in antisemitism, racism, and misogyny. That trial was depicted in the 2016 film *Denial*, which was based on her book *History on Trial: My Day in Court with a Holocaust Denier* (New York: Ecco, 2005). Professor Lipstadt is the author of several other books on the Holocaust, including *The Eichmann Trial* (New York: Schocken, 2011) and *Beyond Belief: The American Press and the Coming of the Holocaust* (New York: Free Press, 1985). Her book *Antisemitism: Here and Now* (New York: Schocken, 2019) provides a captivating analysis of current political trends that bolster prejudice and hostility toward Jews in today's world.

Karma Lowe, Associate Dean, Diversity, Equity and Inclusion,
and Community Engagement, Columbia School of Social Work

Karma Lowe is Associate Dean of Diversity, Equity and Inclusion, and Community Engagement at the Columbia School of Social Work. She has held that position since May 2018, and officially opened the School's Office of Diversity, Equity, and Inclusion. She was previously Director of Enrollment, Student Services, and Financial Aid at CSSW. In her work, she draws on many years of experience conducting workshops and facilitating dialogues on diversity, self-awareness, and critical conversations. Ms. Lowe earned her bachelor's degree in sociology from Columbia University before pursuing a master's in international affairs, specializing in conflict resolution, at Columbia's School of International Affairs (SIPA).

Prof. Jonathan D. Sarna, Joseph H. & Belle R. Braun
Professor of American Jewish History, Brandeis University

Jonathan D. Sarna is University Professor and the Joseph H. & Belle R. Braun Professor of American Jewish History at Brandeis University, where he directs its Schusterman Center for Israel Studies. He is also a past president of the Association for Jewish Studies and Chief Historian of the National Museum of American Jewish History in Philadelphia. Author or editor of more than thirty books on American Jewish history and life, he won six awards for his *American Judaism: A History* (Yale University Press, 2004), including the 2004 Everett Jewish Book of the Year Award from the Jewish Book Council. Sarna is a fellow of the American Academy of Arts and Sciences and of the American Academy of Jewish Research. His books include *When General Grant Expelled the Jews* (New York: Schocken, 2012), *Lincoln and the Jews: A History* (with Benjamin Shapell [New York: Thomas Dunne, 2015]), and an edition of *Cosella Wayne*, by Cora Wilburn (University of Alabama Press, 2019), the first (and hitherto unknown) American Jewish novel.

David Suissa, Editor-in-Chief and Publisher
of the *Los Angeles Jewish Journal*

David Suissa is President of Tribe Media/Jewish Journal, where he has been writing a weekly column on the Jewish world since 2006. In 2015, he was awarded first prize for "Editorial Excellence" by the American Jewish Press Association. Prior to Tribe Media, Suissa was founder and CEO of Suissa Miller Advertising, a marketing firm named Agency of the Year by *USA Today*. He sold his company in 2006 to devote himself full-time to his first passion: Israel and the Jewish world. Suissa was born in Casablanca, Morocco, grew up in Montreal, and now lives in Los Angeles with his five children.

Rachel Wahba, Writer

Rachel Wahba is a writer, psychotherapist, and cofounder of Olivia Travel/Companies. An Iraqi-Egyptian Jew born in India, she grew up in Japan. The many dimensions of displacement and exile are constant themes in her work as a writer and therapist, as well as in her activism as a Mizrahi Jew who grew up stateless.

Rabbi David Wolpe, Max Webb Senior
Rabbi, Sinai Temple, Los Angeles

Named one of the "500 Most Influential People in Los Angeles," the "Most Influential Rabbi in America" by *Newsweek,* and one of the "50 Most Influential Jews in the World" by the *Jerusalem Post*, David Wolpe is the Max Webb Senior Rabbi of Sinai Temple in LA. Rabbi Wolpe previously taught at the Jewish Theological Seminary of America in New York, the American Jewish University in Los Angeles, Hunter College, and UCLA. A columnist for Time.com, he has been published and profiled in the *New York Times, Los Angeles Times, Washington Post*'s "On Faith" website, the *Huffington Post,* and the *New York Jewish Week*. He has been featured on the *Today Show, Face the Nation, ABC This Morning*, and *CBS This Morning*. In addition, Rabbi Wolpe has appeared prominently in series on PBS, A&E, History Channel, and Discovery Channel. Rabbi Wolpe is the author of eight books, including the national bestseller *Making Loss Matter: Creating Meaning in Difficult Times* (New York: Riverhead, 1999). His book *David: The Divided Heart* (New Haven: Yale University Press, 2014) was a finalist for the National Jewish Book Awards and has been optioned for a movie by Warner Bros.

MW00864217